PRAISE FOR

Sue Goetz and *A Taste for Herbs*

"If anyone can take you by the hand and lead you to exciting, delicious and enticing flavors, it's Sue Goetz, the master of herbs and herbal flavorings. Get this book and start your journey to amazing flavor."

> ~ **Shawna Coronado, wellness lifestyle blogger, author of** *The Wellness Garden*

"This fun, informative book will inspire every reader to become an herbal wizard! A must-have for anyone interested in growing and using herbs to enhance our everyday culinary experience."

> ~ **Brie Arthur, author of** *The Foodscape Revolution*

"Sue has a way of blending herbs for flavor that takes your senses to a whole new level. How wonderful that her recipes are available for everyone to try!"

> ~ **Stephanie Rose, GardenTherapy.ca, author of** *Garden Made*

"With a focus on flavor, *A Taste for Herbs* is a thorough primer for choosing, growing and elevating everyday cooking with seasonal herbs."

> ~ **Susan Morrison, landscape designer, author of** *The Less is More Garden*

"Not only does *A Taste for Herbs* give you new ideas about what to do with old favorites, but it is filled with so many beautiful photos that you just want to sit and flip through the pages for hours."

~ **Deborah Niemann, ThriftyHomesteader.com, author of *Homegrown and Handmade***

"Sue's first book, *The Herb Lover's Spa Book*, is one of my favorites, and it remains at fingertip reach as a handy source for all of my herbal spa projects. I'm excited that Sue is once again sharing her expertise and giving us even more recipes and ways to use our favorite plants to enhance our kitchens and daily lives."

~ **Dee Nash, author, writer and editor at Red Dirt Ramblings, author of *The 20-30 Something Garden Guide***

"Sue is the perfect flavour guide to growing and using herbs – from individual flavors to out-of-this-world blends. Let Sue show you how to transform your meals using delicious herbs!"

~ **Niki Jabbour, host of The Weekend Gardener radio show, author of *Veggie Garden Remix***

"*A Taste for Herbs* is everything you could want in a single, useful, beautiful volume."

~ **Ellen Zachos, author of *The Backyard Forager*, BackyardForager.com**

"With Sue's voice in my ear I find myself harvesting, chopping and savoring the fragrance and flavors of the once-ignored herbs growing in my own garden."

~ **Marianne Binetti, TV host, columnist, gardening book author, including *Herb Gardening in Washington and Oregon***

"Wow! … a treasure of simple secrets to prepare and enjoy the taste of your favorite garden herbs."

~ **Ed Hume, founder of Ed Hume Seeds; author, TV host and producer of Gardening in America**

A
TASTE
for
HERBS

A
TASTE
for
HERBS

A guide to seasonings, mixes and blends from the herb lover's garden

Sue Goetz

st. lynn's
press

Pittsburgh

A Taste for Herbs
Your guide to seasonings, mixes and blends from the herb lover's garden

ISBN-13: 978-1-943366-38-5

Library of Congress Control Number: 2018910498
CIP information available upon request

First Edition, 2019

St. Lynn's Press . POB 18680 . Pittsburgh, PA 15236
412.466.0790 . www.stlynnspress.com

Disclaimer:
This book is intended for personal use. All recipes and information are researched for their safe ingredients to consume and use as noted. Recipes in this book regarding health or skin care are for educational purposes only and not intended to diagnose, treat or prevent any disease. All of the herbal information is sourced from reputable research and the author's personal experience and is regarded as safe. Not all health claims made are approved or advised for use by the FDA.

Book design – Holly Rosborough
Editor – Catherine Dees

Photo credits:
All photos © Sue Goetz

Printed in Canada
On certified FSC recycled paper using soy-based inks

This title and all of St. Lynn's Press books may be purchased for educational, business or sales promotional use. For information please write:
Special Markets Department . St. Lynn's Press . POB 18680 . Pittsburgh, PA 15236

10 9 8 7 6 5 4 3 2 1

To my daughters:

Alyssa, Hayley and Courtney

TABLE OF CONTENTS

PART TWO • CREATE!

RESOURCES

INTRODUCTION

I was once asked if I was a foodie and I replied, I think maybe I am. It's just that it sounds so trendy, and sometimes I bristle at something that is ultra-trendy. So, what is a foodie, really? A pretty basic definition would be: a person who likes food, flavor and the process of preparing, cooking and presenting. Okay, that's definitely me. I also like to grow and create most of the flavor enhancers I use in cooking. Considering my appreciation of flavor and taste, I guess you could call me a reluctant foodie, because while I know that main dish recipes are important (of course!), what excites me most is the process of growing and preparing flavor for the main dish.

LOVING FLAVOR

Most important in that definition is the appreciation of flavor and all the things you can add to common ingredients to make them sing. I tend to be an impatient foodie too. I like to prepare fresh food, and I want to be able to grab a seasoning mix out of my cabinet and sprinkle, drizzle, infuse – whatever it takes to add the flavor. So, blending and preserving mixes from my own garden makes sense to me. The recipes you find here are mixes in a ready-to-use form. Many can be stored in the spice cabinet, the refrigerator, or frozen.

This book is all about taste and how flavor – the flavor of herbs – can be used to enrich your experience of eating. It's about creating the tingle on your taste buds. It's about the ancient and beautiful art of seasoning.

But it's about more, especially for anyone who, like me, has experienced health issues and then discovered the "something extra" that herbs can contribute to our wellbeing.

A WELLNESS JOURNEY NOTE

As this book began its early transformation into pages and photos, I collected recipes I have used over the years and even pulled a few of my own herbal concoctions out of my spice cabinet. It was time to write them down and put them into recipe form. At the same time I was also in the midst of medical issues. A battle with fibromyalgia and pain and fatigue in recent years was becoming worse – and I was losing. It had always been just annoyance enough that I didn't do much about it...just lived with it and didn't take care of myself. But the symptoms were starting to affect my everyday life. (No need to go into all those medical details, and I do hate to talk much about it. You know – that personal stuff!)

So I took steps to find a doctor with a different approach than just take higher doses of ibuprofen. After a blood test that showed how haywire I had gotten, we started an elimination diet. (Elimination really shouldn't be paired with the word diet; I prefer to call it my wellness journey.) The wellness part focused on healing and identifying foods that were anti-inflammatory. And a dishearteningly short list it was. At first, I wondered what the heck I could eat, but the reality was, yes, my palette was limited but the flavor part was not!

The grocery store shelves became a lesson in limitations: finding mixes, dressings, etc., without sugar, high fructose corn syrup or some derivative of gluten, soy, and all those binders, fillers and just plain hard to say ingredients. I needed to find organic, and free from possible irritant chemical ingredients that are used in processing and in non-organic food-producing growing practices: all inflammatory ingredients I was trying to avoid.

But back in my kitchen cabinet were mixes I had made from herbs in my garden. Aha, so what I was already doing (making herbal vinegars, oils, seasoning salts) suddenly widened into something really important: bringing healthy, natural flavors to the forefront of my everyday food enjoyment. I focused like a laser on finding and developing herbal recipes that are high in flavor but not in unnecessary, possibly inflammatory ingredients.

Where does all this feed into what you are reading? On the list of good things that I could have as much of as I wanted was – yes – herbs! Fresh, unprocessed, organic ingredients and flavor enhancers that were without things that triggered my multiple sensitivities. It was a real revelation – to not give up on flavor, just give up foods and additives that were making me unhealthy. Here is a journey for you, too. Whatever your sensitivities are, you can tailor flavor to make your own food better.

WHAT'S INSIDE:

In these pages you'll find all you need to know about 20 of the most commonly used and flavor-rich herbs: how to grow them (easy!), the best varieties to choose, what parts to use – plus essential information and tips throughout. I'll take you step-by-simple-step through harvesting and preserving the herbs and capturing all those precious flavors.

And, as promised, there are the recipes! Over 100, showing you how to flavor, mix, mingle and blend herb flavors into almost any meal, from finger foods, main dishes and desserts to infused teas, wines and botanical cocktails.

The big takeaway: You become a creator of flavors. A master of blends. An infusion maven. You deepen your relationship with the plants you bring to your table and the garden that produces them (even if it's only a sunny windowsill or a balcony). You enrich your appreciation of the way Mother Nature gives us not only food to sustain us and keep us healthy, but flavors that give us pleasure and joy. It's a win-win partnership.

I wish you a wonderful adventure into the rich, exciting world of herbs.

https://herbloversgarden.com/

TASTE
the Mixology of Flavor and Food

Is food love or is it necessity? Food is simple. It's fuel for your body, of course. But because of the twists and turns in the personality of taste it becomes a higher subject matter. It's personal, it's emotional – even controversial. Just search the internet for diets...no sugar, no carbs, paleo, you know all the names of eating plans. It's a firestorm of information. It could leave anyone at a loss about what to eat. Is it bad or good? Why do I sometimes crave bad things, but wait – which diet says which food, fat, sugar, etc., is bad or good? No wonder eating plans and diets are such a huge billion dollar industry.

Now, stop for a minute, eat a fresh apple from the garden or a sun-ripened cucumber. It's pure and fresh and based solely on nature's own flavorings. We like to eat food when it tastes good – bottom line. It's satisfying and fills some inner need, whether it's emotional or to regulate our blood sugar. But it tastes good and that's the point.

MYSTERIOUS MIXOLOGY

Why do some foods taste better after we season them? It comes down to the natural mixology of combining scent and taste. Take any recipe for a main dish and note the ingredients. It typically begins with a main ingredient like a meat or a vegetable. The next things listed in the recipe are about adding flavor: the salt, the pepper, the spices. The flavor mix becomes important to that main ingredient, turning something ordinary into a culinary delight. Otherwise it is just a simple cut of meat or a plain vegetable. When fragrant, flavorful ingredients are added they begin to meld and mingle and create aroma. It gets your taste buds watering for a bite.

THE SCIENCE OF TASTE

Oh, those crazy taste buds. This reminds me of biology class in grade school. There was a big drawing of a tongue divided into sections, showing bitter taste bud receptors in the back, sour and salt receptors on the sides and sweet in the front. I remember thinking about it when I tried to swallow a nasty-flavored medicine: *Just get it past the taste buds in the back (or sides), then I don't have to taste it.* It didn't always work. Since then, that old theory of the taste map has been debunked by studies showing that the quality of taste is not restricted to any single area of the tongue, but that all areas of the mouth contain sensors for all kinds of taste. With that understanding, it's even more important to know how we mix flavors together so they are desirable – so when food hits those different receptors it's pure mixology.

The taste of food is about the blending of sweet, sour, salty and bitter in ways that stimulate our taste buds. So how do we approach seasoning food? Interesting question with no right or wrong answer. It is more about an individual taste on the tongue. People perceive flavor differently. My taste is different from yours. I don't like spicy heat; I feel it deadens how food tastes in my mouth – yet I know some who say the hotter the chili pepper or spice in a dish, the better. That's fine. There's room in the flavoring universe for everyone.

PLANT-BASED SEASONINGS

To season food, you need to use a mix of herbs and spices balanced with other elements like oil or vinegar that can be added to a

dish to enhance the flavor. Note the word enhance; not overpower, change or replace, but *enhance*. It's adding something to ordinary food to make it taste yummy, or yummier. In our craving for something to eat, it is usually the seasoning that you are craving – the lemon, the pepper, the salt: the seasoning. And it's how we flavor ordinary food that can be as exciting as the main dish we cook.

When you make your own mixes, you are the quality control expert. Growing and harvesting herbs from your garden gives you control over freshness of the ingredients. You control the source. Blending your own seasonings also allows you to choose ingredients to meet dietary needs like gluten-free, sugar-free or salt restricted. Once you grow and use your own herbs you will never look at store-bought the same way again. Realistically, though, you probably won't be growing every herb or spice mentioned in this book, so for seasoning ingredients that you do purchase, choose sustainably sourced and organic ingredients; they will give you the highest quality and best flavor.

Start in the garden. Grow your favorite herbs. Grow them because you like the flavor, then let your taste buds be your guide. Get up-close and personal with the plants in your garden, their flavors and fragrance. Take a leaf...taste it, smell it, rub the leaf until the oils release on your fingers. You quickly learn to recognize the flavor personality of each one: the pungent herbs like rosemary, where a little measure of fresh rosemary as seasoning goes a long way – or the subtler herbs like marjoram that will smell slightly sweet, yet distinct, like its close relative oregano. Marjoram is so subtle that you will find it in recipes where other spices and herbs won't overpower it. All those aromatics connect back to flavor.

GET TO KNOW THE FLAVOR OF HERBS

In basic recipes that call for a specific herb, you might want to experiment or add more unique flavorings. The best way to do that is to become familiar with the taste and how it blends with other things. The following is a sampler of herbs you are probably already familiar with. How would you put in words the flavor of your favorite herb? This would be a moment I wish these pages were scratch and sniff.

BASIL: a clove-like, anise flavor. Very strong with recognizable pungency.

CHIVES: delicate onion taste. Can be overpowered by strong flavored herbs, so it is best to use as a single herb in recipes to enjoy the oniony flavor.

CILANTRO: strong, lemony-lavender taste. Unique and easily lingers its aroma into other ingredients.

DILL: light, familiar smell of pickles. Delicate flavor, very distinct fragrance.

MARJORAM: mellower, sweeter version of oregano. Can be used as a substitute for parsley or oregano in recipes.

MINT: potent, cool and refreshing. Adds a note of sweetness on the tongue.

OREGANO: strong, aromatic, familiar flavor in Italian cooking.

PARSLEY: mild taste. The flat-leaved variety is more flavorful. Good for adding color in recipe mixes.

ROSEMARY: pine-like taste that holds up strong in cooking and roasting.

SAGE: dry, earthy flavor, familiar in poultry stuffing.

THYME: pungent flavor with an earthy, lemon-peel aroma. Can be used in place of oregano or rosemary.

IN THE GARDEN

Think of your garden as a flavor producer. We know what a fresh vine-ripened tomato tastes like or a fresh-picked strawberry popped in your mouth. The next level of flavor in the garden comes from the parts of the plants we use as seasonings: the leaves, stems and seeds. Essential oils in the plant tissues give off pungent and sweet flavorings. That's where herbs come in. Herb plants grown in the garden are loaded with fragrance. Essential oils can be in the entire plant from the leaves, stems, seeds and right down to the roots. These micro droplets of oil in the plants are made up of chemical combinations that create distinct fragrance and flavor. Nature is a wonderful alchemist.

Let's take a peek at Nature's science at work:

BASIL: In that simple basil leaf you throw in pesto there is camphor, estragole, eugenol, plus a few others. Those components combine to create basil's distinct scent. You often hear basil's flavor described as clove-like. The small, woody seed pod that we know as the spice clove is also heavy in eugenol, so our nose smells that similarity that connects the aroma and flavor back to basil.

TARRAGON, STAR ANISE, FENNEL: Sometimes there are higher percentages of certain organic components that are also in other plants, causing us to smell or taste something similar in two or more herbs – like the licorice taste of tarragon, anise star and fennel. It is the organic compound estragole which is an isomer of anethole. Both have the familiar aroma and are commonly found in plants that taste like licorice. The balance that sets it all apart is that fennel is sweeter in its licorice flavor because it has less of the pungency of estragole than tarragon.

MINT: Fresh mint leaves can have up to 70% menthol in their natural oil. Menthol is a stimulant and causes a sensation of cold in the mouth and on the skin. (The mint in that mojito or mint julep is actually chilling the alcohol for you.) Another bit of flavor magic: Mint alone can be a bit stinging on the tongue because of the high percentage of menthol. But adding sweet flavor to it takes away the sting.

LAVENDER AND LEMON: One of the best examples of how the chemical similarities of plants can affect the flavor of food is the mixing of lavender with lemon. Lavender can be a bit medicinal in taste because of the high camphor notes in the plant's essential oil components. It is earthy, almost a bit musty in flavor. Lemon is high in limonene, which gives us that tart, sour bite on the tongue. Most lavenders (based on the soil they are grown in) have a small percentage of the same component of lemons (limonene). So, there is a small thread of taste and aroma relationship that can enhance each other. Adding lemon to lavender tones down the mustiness and pungency of the camphor, making some culinary lavenders taste sweeter. The acidity of lemon or lime also kicks up flavor when herbs have been simmered or lost some of their flavor strength after harvesting.

Aromatherapists know this by way of healing with essential oils. Mixing one oil with another makes each plant's healing qualities better. But it's important to know the characteristics of each and how they work together. And so it is the same with culinary blending.

TOO MUCH, TOO LITTLE, OR JUST RIGHT?

In culinary blending, mixing salt, vinegars and other strong bases with herbs can enhance the better side of them, or it can go so far as to destroy their flavor. Call it a delicate balance, something you learn very quickly when you've added way too much cilantro or rosemary to something. You've kicked in too much of those essential oils that overpower the taste buds. Fun stuff, really.

Why talk about this in a simple herb flavor book? It's all about mixology and not just throwing this plant with that plant and hoping vinegar makes it better. Take a second look at some of your favorite herbs and what it is you like about them. Sweet? Then they can be used in desserts or fruity infused waters. Spicy hot? Use them in rich meat dishes, sauces, heavy vegetables and meat-based stews. Get to know your favorite herbs and think about the base flavors you are tasting. Becoming familiar with a single herb will help you blend and mix it to your personal taste with other things for a culinary adventure.

I just find it fascinating how those simple plants we call herbs are real powerhouses of flavor. So why not capture that fresh, pure flavor of herbs from the garden and use it to season our food?

Let the mixology begin!

PART ONE

Grow!

ONE

Growing Herbs

20 favorites for every-sized garden...indoors too

I love the details of a garden... how pathways are laid out, the stonework; and the growing, changing, giving parts of a garden, the plants. I especially love the fragrance and flavor of herbs. The wonderful thing is that you don't have to have an enormous plot of land to grow herbs. Your herb garden can be as simple as a container overflowing with mint beside a stately rosemary in pottery. The end goal is that you have gathered plants in your garden that not only delight your senses in the garden, but have multiple uses for you beyond the garden.

HERB GARDEN BASICS
(general garden and growing notes)

SOIL: Herbs in the garden prefer well-draining soil. Organic matter like compost added to the soil helps change the soil's structure and replenishes nutrients important to plant growth. In new beds and open garden areas pile it on deep and till or shovel down at least 8 inches (a good shovel turn). The deeper the amended topsoil the easier it will be for roots to anchor down, take in nutrients, improve drainage and simply make it easier to garden in.

SUNLIGHT: A cultural necessity of an herb garden is that it needs to be in the sunniest spot in the garden. Most herbs prefer full sun or a good quality of warm sun for most of the day. If sun is a challenge, look for microclimates of reflective light and warmth within your garden.

DESIGN: When planning the layout of the herb garden, place taller herbs like dill where they won't shade the other herbs.

CARE: Organic and natural are a must when growing and caring for edibles in the garden. What goes on the plants eventually goes in the body when you eat the plants.

Grow your herbs almost anywhere!

CONTAINER GARDENS

Where no planting beds are available, herbs in pottery will fill the niche for growing your herbs. Look for containers at least 2 feet wide and tall to maximize choices of plants to grow. A large, roomy pot can hold a mix of different herbs or you might plant individual varieties in their own pot – a good idea if you're planting aggressive herbs like mint and oregano, which can quickly take over a space.

INDOORS

Herbs are some of the easiest type of plants to grow in containers so they can easily be grown indoors in a sunny window or on the countertop. All your indoor garden really needs is light, warm temperatures and some humidity. Tips for successful indoor growing:

- Plant the herbs in well-draining pots. Terra cotta pots work well because their porosity allows roots to breathe and not get bogged with moisture.

- Herbs grow best in temperatures around 70° F, so be sure they're not near a cold, drafty window.

- Provide humidity, especially in the winter when a heating system can dry the air. Lightly mist your herb plants daily if needed. Don't saturate the leaves with water, just give them a dewy misting.

- Check the moisture of the pot by touching the surface of the soil; it should be cool and lightly moist. Water when the top inch of soil is starting to dry out. Avoid overwatering, as it is the most common failure of indoor gardens.

WHICH HERBS? To start a windowsill or countertop garden, choose herb varieties that you will use frequently in cooking. You will be inspired to use them if they are available through the year – plus, the ongoing harvest will keep herbs tidy and bushy. Choose varieties that are compact growing, like miniature-leaf basils, parsley and marjoram.

GROW LIGHTS: If you don't have a window with enough sun, place potted herbs on a countertop (in the kitchen if possible to keep them handy for cooking.) Use grow lights under a cabinet or over a shelf on the wall to provide needed light to keep herbs happy and healthy.

Let me get out of the way now and introduce you to the "Top 20" of my favorite herbs. In this chapter you'll find the basic cultural information for each, varieties to look for, the parts of the plant you'll use, harvesting and preserving tips, and advice on using the herb in seasonings and in food and drink preparations.

🌿 BASIL

COMMON NAMES: Basil, sweet basil

BOTANICAL NAME: *Ocimum basilicum*

VARIETIES TO LOOK FOR: Italian, heavily-scented varieties include: 'Genovese', 'Napolitano', 'Greek Windowbox', 'Spicy Globe'. Colorful leaved varieties that add subtle color to liquids, cheeses and butter: 'Dark Opal', 'Red Rubin', 'Purple Ruffles'.

A milder basil with a note of citrus is 'Mrs. Burns' Lemon', a small-leaf basil that is delicate and good used fresh in salads. The Thai basils, which have a slightly subtle "basil" flavor with a hint of licorice to them include: 'African Blue', 'Magic Mountain', 'Siam Queen'.

PART OF THE PLANT USED: Leaves

IN THE GARDEN: Basil is a leafy annual that is easy to start from seed. Grow basil in full sun in well-draining soil that is nourished with compost. Grow in a sunny garden location alongside tomatoes and peppers. The colorful leaved basils, like the variety 'Dark Opal', are a great addition to container gardens. Basil is best planted outside after all danger of frost has passed and nighttime temperatures are consistently above 45° F. The plant will shut down leaf production in cooler temperatures and is prone to rot in wet soils.

Regularly pinch off the flowers during the growing season to encourage bushy, leafy growth. Once basil starts to flower, much of the leaf flavor is lost to the flowers, which are edible but not very palatable.

HARVEST NOTES:
- Basil is best used fresh whenever possible. The desirable basil essence is typically lost during the drying process. In some cases, the leaves need to be dry to use in a recipe, so harvest timing is more important.

- The leaves will be most flavorful in the morning just after the dew dries. Harvest the stems with leaves.

- Gently remove the whole leaves from the stems and place in a single layer on a drying screen.

- When completely dry, store the leaves whole and break them down as needed for use in recipes; this will help preserve the flavor. Basil can also be frozen in ice cubes (see how to freeze herbs on page 82).

FOOD AND FLAVORING: Basil's flavor is best described as a deep, rich, clove-like flavor with undertones of lemon and anise. The large leaves and heavy, fresh flavor are used as the main ingredient in vinegars, oils, and to season and garnish cheese and butter. For a rich, classic pesto, use the true Italian basil varieties like Genovese and Napolitano. You will find basil used many ways, but it has flavor kinship with tomatoes, both fresh and simmered into sauces. (For recipes that use basil, see pages 104, 132, 135, 139 and 146.)

OTHER USES: Healing and aromatic, basil is known as a refreshing and calming herb. It has anti-inflammatory and anti-bacterial properties. Make a strong infusion of basil in warm water, dip a cotton ball in the basil water and smooth over skin to help calm rash and irritations. Drink a cup of basil tea to calm nerves and soothe a stress headache.

Purple Genovese-type basil, 'Amethyst Improved'

Siam Queen Thai Basil

BEE BALM

COMMON NAMES: Bee balm, bergamot, Oswego tea

BOTANICAL NAME: *Monarda* spp.

VARIETIES TO LOOK FOR: There are many species of Monarda and each with varying flavors. *Monarda fistulosa* has a bergamot "Earl Grey"-type of fragrance and flavor and the leaves are good in tea. *Monarda citriodora* is also known as lemon bergamot; its new leaves have a strong lemon aroma that makes an excellent tea. The more commonly grown bee balm, *Monarda didyma*, has tangy flower petals, as well as fragrant leaves. In culinary dishes use varieties with red flowers; they are the ones that have the spiciest flavor. Look for these varieties: 'Gardenview Scarlet', 'Cambridge Scarlet' and 'Violet Queen'. *Monarda citriodora* 'Bergamo' and *Monarda fistulosa* 'Claire Grace' are nice varieties for tea making.

PLANT NOTE: Monarda is not the source of flavor for true Earl Grey tea. True bergamot is *Citrus aurantium* var. *bergamia*. The flavor and fragrance of wild bergamot *(Monarda fistulosa)* is very similar and can be used as a substitute.

PARTS OF THE PLANT USED: Flower petals and leaves

IN THE GARDEN: Most Monardas are perennials that can spread aggressively in moist garden soils. *M. didyma* cultivars do well in partial shade, but need evenly moist, well-draining soil. *M. fistulosa* needs full sun, with moist, well-draining soil. Don't crowd plants in mixed planting beds; some varieties are prone to powdery mildew. The ones I have listed above have been shown to have excellent powdery mildew resistance.

HARVEST NOTES:

- Harvest only young fresh leaves. Older leaves have a rough texture and less flavor.

- Dry the leaves whole on drying screens and store in tightly sealed glass jars.

- To use the edible flowers, use just the petals by gently pulling them out of the center of the flower. The flower petals do not hold their flavor in the drying process, so they are best used fresh.

FOOD AND FLAVORING: Use the brightly-colored flower petals in salads and to flavor and adorn butters and cream cheeses. The leaves of Monarda are tangy and heavy with camphor and make a tingly, refreshing tea. Add the dried leaves to tea mixes to give a deep bergamot aroma. The flavor is especially tasty and enhanced when mixed with citrus-flavored herbs like lemon verbena. (For recipes that use Monarda, see pages 118, 152 and 169.)

OTHER USES: The leaves used in teas are reputed to help ease nausea and aid with digestion. In reference to its common name, bee balm is used as a healing soother for bee stings: Grab a few fresh, tender leaves, crush into a pulp and place at the site of the sting. Bee balm is an excellent pollinator plant in the garden, attracting bees and butterflies. Hummingbirds are highly attracted to the bright-colored flowers.

Gardenview Scarlet *(Monarda didyma)*

Wild Bergamot *(Monarda fistulosa)*

CHAMOMILE

COMMON NAMES: Chamomile, German chamomile, Roman chamomile

BOTANICAL NAME: *Matricaria recutita* (German chamomile), *Chamaemelum nobile* (Roman chamomile)

VARIETIES TO LOOK FOR: Both types of chamomile are used interchangeably in teas and medicine. Roman chamomile has a sweeter, green apple-like aroma and is better used in cooking and teas. Double chamomile (*Chamaemelum nobile* 'Flora Plena') is a lovely double flower form. Bodegold Chamomile (*Matricaria recutita* 'Bodegold') is a variety bred for commercial production because the flowers produce a high-quality essential oil.

PART OF THE PLANT USED: Flowers

IN THE GARDEN: Roman chamomile grows as a low growing, perennial living carpet. It is traditionally used as ground cover in English gardens for pathways and lawns. Grow Roman chamomile as a ground cover under roses; they have a symbiotic relationship that helps keep roses healthy. German chamomile is an annual that grows up to 2 feet tall. Both are easy to plant from seed and will take part-shade with moist, well-draining soil.

HARVEST NOTES:
- Harvest the flowers just as they fully open.
- Dry them on flat drying screens.

FOOD AND FLAVORING: Commonly used for teas. Infuse the fresh flowers in hot water. Use dry flower heads in blends with other herbs, like lavender, for flavorful herb tea mixes. The flowers have a tart, honey-like flavor and can be used fresh in salads and as a garnish for desserts. Chamomile pairs nicely with vanilla flavor for a sweet infusion in cocktails.

An herbal hot toddy for evening relaxation: Make a large cup (8 ounces) of hot, strong chamomile tea. Add 1 teaspoon of honey (see the Chamomile Infused Honey recipe on page 126), a squeeze of fresh lemon juice (about ½ teaspoon), and a shot of rum. Sip and enjoy. (For other recipes that use chamomile see pages 118, 126, 127 and 169.)

OTHER USE: Chamomile is widely respected for it healing qualities. The flowers, when sipped as tea, are calming and help encourage relaxation and sleep. *Chamomile Tea:* Boil water in a teakettle. Transfer boiling water into a warmed glass or ceramic teapot. Add a handful of fresh chamomile flowers and allow to steep for at least 10 minutes, longer for stronger tea.

Chamomile's healing properties are also used for skin care in lotions and shampoos. Harvest fresh flowers and crush into a poultice with a small amount of coconut oil to create a healing mix for skin swelling and irritation. Relax with warm chamomile tea bags over eyes to reduce dark circles and swelling.

 # CHIVES

COMMON NAME: Chives

BOTANICAL NAME: *Allium schoenoprasum* (common chives), *Allium tuberosum* (garlic chives)

VARIETIES TO LOOK FOR: Profusion® chives *(Allium schoenoprasum* 'Sterile') is a cultivar that flowers heavily. Garlic chives *(Allium tuberosum)* are a flat-leaved, white flowering variety.

PARTS OF THE PLANT USED: Stems and flowers.

IN THE GARDEN: A hardy, herbaceous perennial, chives are essential in every chef's herb garden. Chives are not fussy in the garden and do best in well-draining soil in full sun. They can be easily grown from seed. Deadhead faded flower heads to encourage more stem growth through the season. Divide the clumps every 3 or 4 years to keep lush stem and flower production. Chives are also easy to grow inside in a pot on a sunny windowsill.

HARVEST NOTES:

- Harvest fresh for use any time that the plant has matured above ground at least 6 inches. Grasp a handful around the stems and cut, leave at least 2 to 3 inches of the plant behind to regenerate new growth for multiple harvests through the season.

- To dry common chives: Cut the harvested stems into small pieces (about ¼-inch size) and allow to dry on flat drying screens. (The white flowering cultivar known as garlic chives are best used fresh, because they do not stay flavorful in the drying process.)

- To freeze, cut fresh, harvested stems into small pieces, spread in a single layer on a flat baking tray. Place tray in the freezer overnight. Once the chive pieces are frozen, store them in a glass freezer-safe canning jar and cover tightly.

- Chive flowers are best used fresh: You can eat the whole flower head (and a very zingy bite it is) or pull the petals away from the center of the flower head.

FOOD AND FLAVORING: Chives belong to the same plant family as onions and garlic. The flavor of chives is a nice, mild mix of both. Add chives at the end of cooking time, because much of the flavor will be lost in the heat. Sprinkle fresh flower petals and cut stems on all types of salads, soups and savory entrees. Infuse stems and petals into butter and cream cheeses. The dried stems are used in seasoning blends, adding a touch of garlic, without overpowering the mix. The whole flower heads are used in oil or vinegar and will color the liquid a pale lavender-pink. (For recipes that use chives, see pages 106, 108, 112, 134, 142 and 151.)

OTHER USES: Plant chives around roses and nasturtiums to help deter aphids and other garden pests. Garlic chives attract pollinators like bees and butterflies to the garden.

CILANTRO

COMMON NAMES: Cilantro, coriander, Chinese parsley

BOTANICAL NAME: *Coriandrum sativum*

VARIETIES TO LOOK FOR: 'Santo', 'Calypso', and 'Slow Bolt' are cultivars that produce abundant leaves and do not go to seed as quickly as common cilantro.

PARTS OF THE PLANT USED: Fresh leaves. The seeds of the dried fruit of the plant are harvested and commonly known as coriander.

IN THE GARDEN: Cilantro is an annual that changes dramatically in the garden as the temperature rises. This is a cool weather herb; in the summer heat the plant will produce fewer leaves. The stems will lengthen, get thick and begin producing ferny foliage that quickly "bolts" into flower and seed production. The seeds are quick to germinate and like to be consistently moist. I used to plant cilantro seeds in early spring under my greenhouse benches so they could be warm but also shaded, to help the cilantro produce more leaves before it bolted to flower. If you live in an area where danger of frost is late, you can plant a fall crop. Plant seeds so the timing of leaf harvest is about a month from sowing.

HARVEST NOTES:

- Leaves are harvested fresh when young and tender. The older leaves become bitter, when the plant is starting to bolt.

- Gather and cut the stems in a small bunch, then gently tear or snip the leaves from the stems.

- The leaves do not hold flavor well in the drying process. Freeze leaves in ice cubes for later use to melt the flavor into soups and sauces.

- The seeds need to be harvested when fully ripe and dry or the unripe seed will have an unpleasant taste and odor.

FOOD AND FLAVORING: The leaves are pungent and aromatic, described often as lemony, parsley-like. This is a real love it/hate it herb. Some people love the aroma and flavor and some find it repulsive. It is a savory herb that has flavor power in heavy dishes and one of the popular ingredients in salsa recipes. Use this herb lightly so it does not overpower dishes, but daintily lends its distinct flavor. Typically, when a recipe calls for coriander (and not cilantro) it is referring to the use of the seed. The seeds are used as one of the main ingredients in curry powder. (For recipes that use cilantro and coriander, see pages 106 and 148.)

OTHER USES: Coriander seed is a botanical addition for flavor in gin making. A fascinating component of coriander seed is that in testing it is made up of over 70% linalool, which is a naturally occurring terpene alcohol. That heavy amount of linalool makes the fresh aromatic oil of coriander, popular for use commercially as a base in perfumes and lotions.

 # DILL

COMMON NAME: Dill

BOTANICAL NAME: *Anethum graveolens*

VARIETIES TO LOOK FOR: 'Mammoth' is a plume of soft foliage that grows up to 3 feet tall. 'Bouquet' is a compact-growing dill. 'Dukat' is popular because of its strong flavor that holds well in cooking. 'Fernleaf' is a compact-growing plant that works great in potted herb gardens.

PARTS OF THE PLANT USED: Leaves and seeds

IN THE GARDEN: Dill is an annual that is easy to grow from seed. It prefers full sun and well-draining soil. Plant dill in early spring, about the same time you would plant cool crops like lettuce. Sow a second or third time every couple of weeks to have a continual harvest of leaves. Allow some of the plant to flower to be harvested for the seed. You can also plant a later crop to have fresh dillweed sprigs for pickle making.

HARVEST NOTES:

- Harvest dill weed (the leaves) through the summer for fresh use. The seeds are ready to harvest just as they are turning brown.

- To harvest seeds, cut the flower/seed heads from the plants, keeping some length of stems. Tie the bundle together with string or a rubber band and cover it with a brown paper bag.

- Hang the bag to finish drying. As the seed dries, it will shake off the plant into the paper bag.

- Store the seeds in a glass jar.

FOOD AND FLAVORING: The ferny-textured leaf of dill is commonly referred to in recipes as dill weed. It has the familiar flavor of dill pickles but more subtle than dill seed. Add dill leaves near the end of cooking time to delicate-flavored dishes with chicken or fish.

Add to baby salad greens, sprinkle on fresh sliced cucumbers, season cream cheese, butter and egg dishes. The aromatic seeds attached to the umbel flowers have a stronger flavor. This is the part of the plant used in pickles. The strong flavor retains well in vinegars and as a flavorful addition to baked breads. (For recipes that use dill, see pages 104, 108, 140 and 152.)

OTHER USES: Dill is a prized pollinator garden plant; it is a host plant for swallowtail butterflies. *Dill tea – a tea made with the seeds will help ease stomach gas and upset:* Infuse one teaspoon of seeds into 1 cup of hot water and allow to steep for about 15 minutes. Dill has also been studied as an immune system booster and found to have anti-inflammatory qualities.

 **FENNEL**

COMMON NAMES: Fennel, sweet fennel, Florence fennel

BOTANICAL NAME: *Foeniculum vulgare*

VARIETIES TO LOOK FOR: Sweet fennel *(Foeniculum vulgare)*, bronze fennel *(Foeniculum vulgare* 'Rubrum'*)*, Florence fennel *(Foeniculum vulgare* var. *azoricum)*, 'Romanesco' or 'Victorio'.

PARTS OF THE PLANT USED: Leaves and seeds of sweet and bronze varieties. The bulb of Florence fennel.

IN THE GARDEN: Sweet fennel and bronze fennel are easily grown from seed. The plant prefers full sun with consistent moisture in well-draining soil. Plants don't like to be crowded, so keep them thinned to about 10 to 12 inches apart from each other. Fennel can be a bit invasive and is showing up on noxious weed lists across the country. (Check with your county extension agent if it is a problem in your area.) Cut the flower heads from the plant before they seed to keep it from self-sowing around the garden. Bronze fennel has dark, lacy foliage that adds nice texture to container gardens. Plant fennel seeds in the garden when the soil warms in the spring. The variety commonly known as Florence fennel produces a large, bulb-like base. Plant Florence fennel seed with a spacing of 12 inches, to give room for the bulb to grow. The plants need a long season and rich well-draining soil to produce a nice bulb. For the bulb type of fennel start seeds indoors and place plants out in the garden in the spring as soon as the danger of frost has passed.

HARVEST NOTES:

- Harvest the feathery leaves anytime for fresh use.
- Harvest the flower and seed heads to dry using the same method as dill.

- The bulb of Florence fennel is ready to harvest when the bulb is about the size of a tennis ball. If the bulb gets too big and mature, it may become stringy with an unpleasant texture.

FOOD AND FLAVORING: Fennel is very recognizable by its strong anise fragrance and flavor. The chopped leaves are used on fish and do particularly well to improve the digestibility of oily fish. Use fennel leaves in soups, stews and salad. Fennel seeds can be used as a substitute for anise seed in recipes. The taste is milder but still imparts the licorice-like scent and flavor. Sauté the seeds in stir-fry and rice dishes. The seeds are a main flavoring used in Italian sausage making. The bulbous base of Florence fennel can be sliced raw for use in leaf lettuce salads. Sauté large pieces of the bulb in butter to impart an anise flavor; add shrimp, green beans or peas pods for a sweet, mellow dish. (For recipes that use fennel, see pages 108 and 180.)

OTHER USES: The seed of sweet fennel is long revered as a stomach calmer. *Fennel tea:* Add 1 teaspoon of fennel seeds to 1 cup of boiling water. Crush the seeds slightly while in the hot water and allow to steep for 1 minute. Strain the tea before drinking and garnish with a fresh slice of orange. The infusion can also be used as a mouthwash or a gargle to calm a sore throat. The seeds are used to flavor liquors and candy. In the garden the umbel-shaped flowers are one of the important host plants for swallowtail butterflies.

Bronze Fennel
(Foeniculum vulgare dulce 'Rubrum')

41

✹ LAVENDER

COMMON NAME: Lavender

BOTANICAL NAME: *Lavandula* spp.

VARIETIES TO LOOK FOR: There are hundreds of varieties of lavender to choose from. For the best taste, the English varieties and a few hybrids are the ones to grow for flavor. Generally, the darker the flower color of the *Lavandula angustifolia* varieties the sweeter the flavor. Look for 'Hidcote', 'Munstead', 'Royal Velvet', and 'Sachet'. 'Melissa' is a pale pink flowering cultivar that has a nice sweet flavor. The Lavandins *(Lavandula* x *intermedia)* 'Grosso, 'Provence', 'Seal' are larger plants and heavy flower producers.

PART OF THE PLANT USED: Flower buds

IN THE GARDEN: Lavender is a sun-loving perennial. The English lavenders are hardy to USDA Zones 5 or 6 with the variety 'Munstead' being one of the hardiest and will survive USDA Zone 4 winters. The hybrid Lavandins are less hardy and do best in USDA Zone 6 to 10. All lavenders dislike nourished soil; garden ground that is heavily composted or too rich may grow healthy plants but will not have good flower production. Plant lavender in rocky, lean soil. Good drainage is imperative to avoid root rot. In rainy climates, especially those with cool, wet winters, top dress around the base of the plants with white gravel or oyster shells to keep the foliage from lying in wet soil. If the flowers are cut or sheared back after they fade in mid-summer, the plants tend to have a second flush of flowers later in the season.

HARVEST NOTES:

- The stems of lavender are best harvested when the light-gray color of the still-closed flower buds begin to deepen in color to purple. This is the maturity stage just before the bud opens into petal. Some of the lower petals on the stem may be open, but the best essential oil is in the plump and colorful bud.

- Fresh use: Cut from the garden, the buds can be gently stripped from the stems.

- To dry: Cut long stems with flower buds and bind them together into bundles with a rubber band.

- Hang to dry, keep a watch on the drying bundles before the buds begin to shatter off. To catch the buds as they are drying, you can enclose the bundle in a paper bag, as the flower buds shatter off they will fall into the bottom (see the paper bag method in the general harvest section.)

- When the buds are completely dry, shake them from the stems and store them in a glass jar.

FOOD AND FLAVORING: Lavender has an earthy, sweet, perfume flavor. The English lavenders have the sweetest flavor, perfect for desserts, jellies and cocktails. The Lavandins have higher notes of camphor and menthol, giving them a more pungent aroma that combines with pepper and savory seasonings. Use fresh stems of lavender in bud as swizzle sticks in cocktails and summer drinks. Lavender mixed with lemon in recipes makes the lavender taste better because the essential oils in the plants contain small amounts of limonene, which is the same component that gives lemon its classic fresh fragrance. (For recipes that use lavender, see pages 102, 118, 121, 125, 128, 164 and 165.)

Hidcote Lavender (*Lavandula angustifolia* 'Hidcote')

OTHER USES: Lavender in the garden is a bee attractant and thrives in hot, sunny, drought-tolerant gardens. Lavender buds, when infused in bathing mixes and lotions, are healing and calming to damaged or irritated skin. It also helps ease a migraine: Make a headache-relieving compress: Add about 5 tablespoons of lavender buds per cup of water and make a strong water infusion. Allow the water to cool to room temperature. Immerse a cotton washcloth in the lavender water and wring out the excess. Fold the cloth, place across forehead and relax for 15 minutes or longer.

🌿 LEMON VERBENA

BOTANICAL NAME: *Aloysia triphylla*

VARIETIES TO LOOK FOR: Lemon verbena

PART OF THE PLANT USED: Leaves

IN THE GARDEN: Lemon verbena is a woody, shrubby plant that can grow up to 8 feet tall. It is tender to frost and is treated as an annual below USDA Zone 9. Grows best in full sun and with regular water. Start the plants in the garden from cuttings, because it does not propagate reliably from seed. Keep the flowers cut during the growing season to encourage full, bushy leaf growth. In an area where the plant is tender, they can be overwintered in a greenhouse to protect from frost. When moved indoors, the plant will tend to drop all their leaves during colder periods. The bare wood stems will re-sprout leaves if kept watered, and as daylight hours increase in the spring.

HARVEST NOTES:
- Harvest the leaves for fresh use anytime. They are most pungent when fresh.
- To dry: Cut the woody stems with leaves still attached; bundle and hang to dry. When the leaves begin to curl and are completely dry, gently strip the leaves from the stems and store them whole until ready to use.
- The fresh leaves can also be pulled off the woody stems and dried flat on screens.

FOOD AND FLAVORING: This plant is an herb garden essential, even in areas when it is tender. The fresh leaves have an irresistible, sweet, lemon drop fragrance. Use them as a garnish on desserts and beverages. Infuse the leaves into liquids for cordials and sugar syrups. Add fresh, chopped leaves to cookies, cakes muffins and ice cream. Yummy addition to homemade jams: Add small tender leaves pinched from the top of branches to peach jam as it simmers and begins to thicken.

Lemon verbena is a favorite tea herb, use the leaves dried in blends. *For sun tea:* Fill a gallon glass jar half-full with fresh harvested lemon verbena leaves, add a few sprigs of fresh mint and allow to steep in the hot sun for about 4 to 6 hours. Strain off the leaves, add lemon verbena ice cubes and garnish with sliced lemons for a refreshing drink. (For other recipes that use lemon verbena, see pages 113, 118, 122, 135, 152, 163, 169, 179 and 180.)

OTHER USES: Lemon verbena leaf tea is used to calm indigestion and stomach cramps. The plant and essential oil used in soap is soothing and cleansing to skin. Try this recipes for a relaxing tub soak. *Lemon verbena Epsom bath soak*: 1 cup Epsom salt, ½ cup sea salt and ¼ cup lemon verbena leaves (slightly crushed to fit in the measuring cup). Mix together all ingredients and crush the leaves into the salts with a mortar and pestle until well mixed. Add mixture to a warm bath.

🌿 MARJORAM

COMMON NAMES: Marjoram, sweet marjoram

BOTANICAL NAME: *Origanum majorana*

VARIETIES TO LOOK FOR: Variegated marjoram *(Origanum vulgare* 'Variegata')

PART OF THE PLANT USED: Leaves

IN THE GARDEN: Marjoram is a tender perennial that is grown as an annual in USDA zones below 8. The leaves of marjoram are small, round and crinkly. The flowers have a distinctive appearance as little rounded "knots" arranged around the taller stems. It is a low (about 12 to 18 inches) spreading plant that does best in full sun in well-draining soil.

HARVEST NOTES:

- Harvest leaves individually for fresh use during the season.

- To dry: Grasp a bunch of stems on the plant and cut the stems approximately 4 to 6 inches from the ground.

- Strip off lower leaves and wrap the base of the bundle with a rubber band or string and hang to dry.

- After the bundles are dry, strip the leaves off the stems and store in a glass jar.

FOOD AND FLAVORING: Marjoram is closely related to oregano and has a similar, milder flavor but with a note of sweetness. Marjoram can be substituted for oregano, just double the measure of marjoram to add more pungency. The flowery flavor is good to use in pasta salads and added to spring green salads. The dried leaves add a spicy sweetness to seasoning salts and grilling rubs. (For recipes that use marjoram, see pages 131, 133, 147 and 172.)

OTHER USES: The tops of the plants can be used to dye fabric in shades of yellow or orange. Marjoram is popular to use in perfumery as a spicy base note that blends but does not overpower other aromas. Taken as a warm tea it is reputed to help ease cold symptoms, anxiety and insomnia.

Variegated Marjoram *(Origanum vulgare* 'Variegata'*)*

 **MINT**

COMMON NAME: Mint

BOTANICAL NAME: *Mentha* spp.

VARIETIES TO LOOK FOR: Moroccan mint, spearmint, chocolate mint, 'Kentucky Colonel', 'Swiss', apple mint, Mojito mint, pineapple mint.

PART OF THE PLANT USED: Leaves

IN THE GARDEN: Mint is one of the easiest herbs to grow and produces abundant leaves for a long season of fresh cutting. Most mint does not tend to grow true from seed; propagate from a plant you know has good flavor or buy plants from an herb grower. Mints prefer moist soils and grow best in full sun. Because mint can be a rampant spreader in the garden, grow the plants in container gardens to help control its spreading habit. The plants can become root bound in a pot over one season and will need to be divided and repotted to keep them from dying out in the center of the plant. Cut the plants back regularly: the new leaves will have a stronger mint flavor than older leaves.

HARVEST NOTES:

- Harvest whole fresh leaves through the season. Dry leaves on drying screens.
- Store them whole to preserve the flavor.
- Don't crush or tear them until you are ready to add to a recipe.

FOOD AND FLAVORING: True peppermint is one of the stronger-flavored varieties, while spearmint, Moroccan mint and chocolate mint tend to have a sweeter flavor. 'Swiss' mint and the fruit-scented varieties are milder. Mint is used in numerous dishes both savory and sweet. Use as a garnish on desserts and beverages. Add to rice and vegetable dishes to add a tangy note. Dried mint leaves with a twist of crystalized lemon or lime add zing to seasoning salts and meat-grilling rubs. Keep a good supply of mint ice cubes in the freezer for use in water bottles and iced beverages. (For recipes that use mint, see pages 118, 120, 153, 162, 163, 169, 173, 177 and 180.)

OTHER USES: Peppermint oil is one of the most popular essential oils. Extracted from the leaves, it is used in chewing gum and candies as well as body care products like soap, toothpaste, shampoos and lotions. The heavy concentration of menthol in the plant oil is also used as a local anesthesia. A warm tea made from the leaves will help soothe nausea and help to digest foods after a heavy meal.

OREGANO

COMMON NAME: Oregano

BOTANICAL NAME: *Origanum vulgare*

VARIETIES TO LOOK FOR: True Greek oregano, 'Hot and Spicy', 'Kaliteri'

IN THE GARDEN: Oregano is an herbaceous, spreading perennial. It thrives in a sunny location in well-draining rocky soil. It tends to spread around in the garden but does not do well in containers, so give it room to grow and divide it every few years to keep it in check.

PART OF THE PLANT USED: Leaves

HARVEST NOTES:
- Use the leaves fresh or dried. To harvest, cut stems approximately 4 to 6 inches from the ground.
- Strip off lower leaves and bundle with a rubber band or string and hang to dry.
- After the bundles are dry, strip the leaves off the stems and store in a glass jar.

FOOD AND FLAVORING: Oregano is popular in pizza and Italian dishes because its familiar aroma holds well in baking and simmering. Oregano varieties can differ in how peppery and strong they taste. In cooking, the white-flowering Greek oregano has the best peppery zing. Dry the Greek varieties for use in seasoning blends. Knead a tablespoon of finely chopped oregano into homemade bread or pizza dough. Use fresh oregano as the main ingredient in pesto for a pungent spread to use on crackers or pita chips served with sliced tomatoes and mozzarella cheese. (For recipes that use oregano, see pages 99, 104, 108, 110, 112 and 146.)

OTHER USES: Grow golden oregano (*Origanum vulgare* 'Aureum') for its beauty in the landscape. The small, golden, crinkled leaves have a low spreading habit that adds

Golden Oregano *(Origanum vulgare* 'Aureum'*)*

foliage color to rock gardens. Hopley's Purple *(Origanum laevigatum)* has deep burgundy-colored flower heads and long stems that are beautiful in flower arrangements. Oregano has a long-standing healing tradition as an anti-inflammatory and pain killer.

❧ PARSLEY

COMMON NAME: Parsley

BOTANICAL NAME: *Petroselinum crispum*

VARIETIES TO LOOK FOR: Moss Curled *(Petroselinum crispum crispum)* is a bright green curly variety. Triple-curled is a nice heirloom variety with extra curly leaves that form attractive lacy, thick mounds. Italian parsley *(Petroselinum crispum neapolitanum)* is a favorite culinary choice.

PART OF THE PLANT USED: Leaves

IN THE GARDEN: Parsley is an easy herb to start from seed. It prefers to grow in full sun with evenly moist, well-draining soil. Parsley is a biennial and will produce abundant leaves the first year and grow flower stems and go to seed in the second growing season.

HARVEST NOTES:
- Cut the fresh stems at the base of the plant with leaves attached for use as needed. To help retain vitamins and other nutrient values, don't cut or tear the leaves until you are ready to add them to a recipe.
- Harvest before the plant goes into flower and seed to avoid bitter-tasting leaves.
- Dry the leaves on screens and store whole.
- Chopped parsley can be frozen on a baking sheet or in ice cubes.

FOOD AND FLAVORING: The fresh flavor of curly parsley leaves is a good addition to salads, including cold pasta. Place the leaves on sandwiches like you use lettuce. Makes an excellent pesto to serve with crackers and salami. The Italian flat-leaved variety has a more intense flavor than the common curly variety and will hold up to dishes that are heated. Parsley is a must in tabbouleh recipes to keep the traditional flavor. Dried parsley adds an "herb" garden flavor to seasoning salts. For color appeal and full flavor, add fresh parsley leaves as a finishing garnish. If added during cooking, the heat will cause a chemical reaction in fresh parsley and the leaves may turn an unappetizing brown color. Here's a smelly cooking tip: if you've added too much onion or garlic to a recipe, stir in some parsley; it will absorb and tone down the flavor and odor. (For recipes that use parsley, see pages 104, 107, 108, 112, 133, 134 and 146.)

OTHER USES: Parsley is a good green boost to add to smoothies; the fresh leaves are loaded with vitamins, beta-carotene and iron. Chew fresh curled parsley leaves for a quick breath freshener. Infuse leaves into water and use as a skin tonic. Wipe irritated skin with a cotton ball soaked in parsley water to soothe and calm irritation.

Moss Curled Parsley *(Petroselinum crispum* 'Moss Curled'*)*

🌿 ROSEMARY

COMMON NAME: Rosemary

BOTANICAL NAME: *Rosmarinus officinalis*

VARIETIES TO LOOK FOR: 'Arp', 'Barbeque', 'Gorizia', 'Spice Island', 'Tuscan Blue'

PART OF THE PLANT USED: Leaves

IN THE GARDEN: Rosemary is a perennial evergreen hardy in USDA Zone 7 and above. Grow as an annual in containers in climates where it is tender. The variety 'Arp' is one of the hardiest and may overwinter in USDA Zones 5 or 6. Rosemary is native to the hot wind-swept hills of Mediterranean regions of the world. Find a spot in the garden that mimics those conditions: full, warm sun and rocky well-draining soil. Inside the home, on a sunny windowsill, a rosemary plant will thrive if kept evenly moist in a well-draining pot – not too much water, not too little. Allow the soil to dry between watering.

HARVEST NOTES:

- Harvest for fresh use any time. Rosemary is best if harvested when the plant is not in flower.

- To dry: Cut long branches and bundle with a rubber band and hang to dry. As the leaves dry they will shatter easily, so use the paper bag drying method to catch the drying leaves.

- When the bundles are completely dry, strip them off the stems and store in a glass jar.

FOOD AND FLAVORING: Rosemary has a pine-like scent. The plant is heavy with essential oils that remain pungent through baking and simmering. Season lightly with rosemary, because it infuses its strong flavor and aroma through recipe ingredients and can easily overpower. The new, tender leaf growth at the ends of branches has the best flavor and tends to be less heavy in the medicinal taste of camphor. The tougher leaves can be simmered as a whole sprig to permeate a dish with flavor; just remove the sprig before serving. Crushed or powdered dried rosemary is good to use in mixes with other strong flavors like smoked salts and chilis. Rosemary is also a good seasoning for fatty meats and seafood. Cut long, straight lengths of fresh branches to use as skewers for meat and vegetables. Sharpen one end of the stem to easily slide on seafood, chicken or meats to make kebabs. (For recipes that use rosemary, see pages 99, 110, 114, 123, 145, 146 and 177.)

OTHER USES: Rosemary has antibacterial properties. *Make an eco-friendly counter cleaner:* You'll need a large bundle of fresh-picked rosemary (add fresh thyme and sage if you have some) and household white vinegar. Gently wash herbs, remove any discolored, damaged leaves and stems. Pack the fresh rosemary, stems and all, into a clean, sterilized glass quart-sized wide-mouth canning jar. Pour the vinegar over the herb. With a wooden spoon (do not use metal utensils) push on the plants to help gently crush and bruise them and release their essential oils into the vinegar. Cover the top of the jar and rim with parchment or plastic wrap, then screw on the lid. Shake well and allow to steep for a week in a cool, dark place. Strain

Tuscan Blue Rosemary *(Rosmarinus officinalis 'Tuscan Blue')*

out all remnants of herb leaves and pour into a spray bottle. Spray and wipe countertops to clean and disinfect them.

🌿 SAGE

COMMON NAMES: Sage, garden sage

BOTANICAL NAME: *Salvia officinalis*

VARIETIES TO LOOK FOR: Salvia is a huge genus of herbal and ornamental plants. For culinary purposes, get picky and choose these for best flavor: common garden sage *(Salvia officinalis)*, 'Berggarten', purple sage *(Salvia officinalis* 'Purpurea'), golden sage *(Salvia officinalis* 'Aurea'), 'Tricolor'

PARTS OF THE PLANT USED: Leaves and flowers

IN THE GARDEN: Sage thrives in warm, sunny areas. It prefers soil on the dry side. The leaves can be harvested year-around in mild climates, where it remains evergreen. Regular cutting and trimming of the plant will help to keep it from getting woody and falling open in the center.

HARVEST NOTES:

- The young, tender leaves at the growing tips of the stems have better flavor, not as heavy and resinous as the older, rougher leaves.
- Cut woody stems and bundle. Hang dry.
- Removes dried leaves and store them whole in glass jars.
- Harvest flowers for fresh use.

FOOD AND FLAVORING: The more flavorful sages for cooking are the large rounded leaf, traditional garden sage. The purple leaf variety lends beautiful color to fresh salads. The leaves are used to flavor cheese, pork sausage and fatty, heavy-flavored meats. It is most

Variegated Berggarten Sage *(Salvia officinalis* 'Berggarten Variegated'*)*

recognized as a seasoning mixed with onion for stuffing turkey and other game birds. Use sage sparingly until you become familiar with its deep, musky flavor. It can easily overpower a recipe. The flowers of sage can be used as a garnish on roasted meats. (For recipes that use sage, see pages 107 and 110.)

OTHER USES: Sage is well known as an antiseptic cleansing herb. Infuse the leaves in water to create a strong brew. Gargle to soothe sore throat. Like many other pungent Mediterranean herbs planted in the garden, deer stay away. Plant a hedge of sage around roses to keep deer from eating all the blossoms.

🌿 SAVORY

COMMON NAMES: Savory, winter savory, summer savory

BOTANICAL NAME: *Satureja* spp.

VARIETIES TO LOOK FOR: There are two types of savory: summer savory *(Satureja hortensis)* and winter savory *(Satureja montana)*. For culinary use, the summer savory is preferred. It has a lighter, less heavy flavor than winter savory.

PART OF THE PLANT USED: Leaves

IN THE GARDEN: Summer savory is an annual and is easily grown from seed. Sow seeds in the spring about the same time you are planting lettuce or after risk of frost. Keep the plants trimmed and flowers removed throughout the growing season to help the plant stay vigorous and less likely to flop over. Winter savory is a low-growing, woody perennial that prefers rocky, well-draining soil in full sun.

HARVEST NOTES:

- You can begin harvesting summer savory when the plants are at least 6 inches tall. Use fresh leaves of summer savory because they do not hold flavor after they are dried.

- Winter savory can be cut and dried. The heavy flavor is better in the drying process than summer savory.

- Cut stems from the plant to create small bundles. Leave about a third of the plant behind to stimulate new growth.

FOOD AND FLAVORING: The name savory is a good descriptor of its flavor. Deep and flavorful, and leaves a bit of hot spicy flavor on the tongue. Savory tastes like a combination of oregano and thyme. The essential oils of savory and thyme are very similar in their chemical makeup so their flavor can be used interchangeably in recipes. Both winter and summer savory taste alike, but winter savory will be stronger and can be used in cooking and simmering without losing its flavor. Store-bought savory is typically only the summer savory. As with other robust-flavored herbs like oregano, rosemary and sage, get familiar with the strong flavor of savory and use it lightly. It can easily overpower other ingredients. Commonly used in German cuisine for flavoring sausages, sauerkraut and meats. (For a recipe that uses savory, see page 146.)

OTHER USES: The essential oil of savory is distilled from the leaves and is very high in phenols; those compound phenols are highly antiseptic. A strong infusion of savory tea can be used to cleanse mild cuts and burns on skin. Savory blended in soap with citrus is highly cleansing and refreshing.

Winter Savory *(Satureja montana)*

SCENTED GERANIUM

COMMON NAME: Scented geranium

BOTANICAL NAME: *Pelargonium* spp.

VARIETIES TO LOOK FOR: These are not the common garden flowering "geranium." Scented geraniums are classified as Pelargoniums. Not all scented Pelargoniums are good for culinary purposes. Choose these selected few for best flavor: 'Attar of Roses', Old fashioned rose, 'Lady Plymouth'

(Peppermint rose). 'Mabel Grey' has an intense lemon aroma and bitter lemon peel type of flavor.

PART OF THE PLANT USED: Leaves

IN THE GARDEN: To stay true to the fragrance and flavor, scented geraniums are best propagated from cuttings rather than seed. Most varieties are tender to frost, with the rose fragrances being the hardiest. For successful growing, scented geraniums need to be in full sun and rich soil. Keep the plants evenly moist, but not soaked. They make a good container plant. Choose large, well-draining pots. Scented geraniums are fast growing and need room in the root area to avoid becoming root bound before the end of the season. In cooler climates, overwinter them in a protected area. They will take a light frost but not ongoing freezing temperatures. Indoors, they can be grown in a warm sunny window.

HARVEST NOTES:
- Harvest leaves for fresh use anytime.
- The leaves will dry well and keep their aroma, but much of the actual flavor is lost in the drying process.

FOOD AND FLAVORING: For culinary uses, the rose varieties are used to impart an earthy flavor and aroma to sweet breads, cakes, teas and jellies. The unique leaves are used as a garnish and can be sugared to decorate desserts and cream pies. *Easy scented* *geranium jelly:* 1 pint of prepared apple jelly and 3 fresh leaves of rose scented geranium. Heat the jelly slowly over a low heat until liquefied. Add 2 rose geranium leaves and stir. Remove from heat. Let sit for 5 minutes. Remove the leaves. In a clean, sterilized jelly jar, place a fresh geranium leaf in the bottom. Pour jelly over the leaf. Allow to cool, cover and refrigerate. Yummy on plain pound cake or warm scones. Keep the jelly refrigerated and try to use within a few weeks. The lemon-scented variety 'Mabel Grey' is best for tea and the leaves can be dried for tea blends. (For other recipes that use scented geranium, see pages 118 and 122.)

OTHER USES: In temperate climates they can be grown in the landscape along borders and pathways to create texture and garden aromatherapy. A cup of rose-scented leaves in infusion is said to reduce stress. Macerate leaves from the cultivar 'Lady Plymouth' (Peppermint rose) into coconut oil to create a soothing lotion for sore joints and aching muscles.

Pelargonium 'Lady Plymouth'

SWEET WOODRUFF

COMMON NAME: Sweet woodruff

BOTANICAL NAME: *Galium odoratum*

VARIETIES TO LOOK FOR: Common sweet woodruff

PARTS OF THE PLANT USED: Leaves and flowers

IN THE GARDEN: Sweet woodruff is a low-growing perennial groundcover that grows well in the shade. It has a sweet vanilla-like fragrance and delicate star-shaped white flowers in early summer. It will spread in moist soils. Use caution because it can become invasive.

HARVEST NOTES:

- Harvest leaves and flowers for fresh use.
- Whole stems with leaves can be dried.
- To dry: Cut stems anytime they are fresh and green, and lay in a single layer on drying screens.

FOOD AND FLAVORING: Sweet woodruff is used in the traditional German drink Maybowl (Maibowle), a mix of sweet woodruff, dry white wines and brandy served on May Day. Cut fresh sprigs of leaves and flowers, remove from the stems and toss with fresh-cut fruits like strawberries and melons. The fresh leaves do not have a strong fragrance, but as they dry they have a delicate honey vanilla fragrance that blends well in tea mixes. (For recipes that use sweet woodruff, see pages 118 and 174.)

OTHER USES: Woodruff is noted in many historical herbals for its healing qualities. Gerard's herbal (1597) describes it as an herb that "...is reported to be put into wine, to make a man merry and to be good for the heart and liver." Woodruff 's sweet aroma when dried is popular in fragrant potpourri mixes and as a filling for sleep pillows.

🌿 TARRAGON

COMMON NAMES: Tarragon, French tarragon

BOTANICAL NAME: *Artemisia dracunculus*

VARIETIES TO LOOK FOR: Choose only true tarragon; it is the only one with the distinct flavor.

PART OF THE PLANT USED: Leaves

IN THE GARDEN: True tarragon does not propagate from seed. You will need to purchase plants from an herb grower or propagate from cuttings. Look for plants with glossy, narrow leaves that emit a sweet licorice aroma when rubbed. Taste a leaf before buying, as some plants are sold as tarragon, but are not true to the flavor of *Artemisia dracunculus*. Tarragon has a rangy, almost weedy habit, but will have a nice bushier shape if grown in hot sun and well-draining soil. Cut regularly to encourage new leaf growth. Do not add compost or too much nourishment or the plant will fall open in the center. Grows best in USDA Zones 4 to 7. Tarragon will also do well indoors on a sunny windowsill.

HARVEST NOTES:

- The leaves are used fresh. For best flavor, pick the leaves before the plant flowers.
- To preserve, the leaves can be infused into liquids or ice cubes.
- Drying is not recommended; the essential oils in the leaves evaporate quickly, making them flavorless.
- Keep flowers trimmed through the growing season to encourage the plant to get bushier.

FOOD AND FLAVORING:
Tarragon has a very distinct flavor. The essential oil's main ingredient is estragole, which smells and tastes like licorice. The most popular use of tarragon leaves is infused into vinegar and oils for use in dressing mixes, and to marinate lighter meats like pork and chicken. The leaves give flavor to mixes for use as a salt substitute. Favored in French cuisine, it is one of the herbs (blended with parsley, chervil, marjoram and chives) in fines herbes bundles. (For recipes that use tarragon, see pages 134 and 155.)

OTHER USES: Seventeenth century herbalist John Evelyn wrote of tarragon: "Tis highly cordial and friend to the head, heart and liver". Modern-day herbalists recommend chewing raw tarragon leaves to help with digestion. It is said to help stimulate appetite.

THYME

COMMON NAME(S): Thyme, common thyme, garden thyme

BOTANICAL NAME: *Thymus* spp.

VARIETIES TO LOOK FOR: As with other herb varieties, there are many cultivars of thyme available. The best ones for cooking and flavor include: English thyme, French thyme, Silver thyme, variegated lemon thyme, 'Orange balsam'.

PARTS OF THE PLANT USED: Leaves, flowers and tender stems

IN THE GARDEN: Upright thyme is a rounded perennial that grows to about 12 to 18 inches tall. Best in full sun and well-draining rocky soil. Trim the leaves regularly to keep the shrub bushy and help prevent it from becoming woody.

HARVEST NOTES:

- Since thyme is low-growing, the cut stems will be small. Grasp a small bunch and cut from plant. Plants can be trimmed to about 3 inches from the ground.

- Thyme is used fresh or dried.

- Place stems in a single layer on drying screens. When completely dry, store the stems and leaves whole. Crumble for use just before cooking.

- To make thyme ice cubes, harvest fresh, tender stems, cut into small pieces and add to ice cube trays. Cover with water and freeze.

FOOD AND FLAVORING: Thyme is a popular herb used in bouquet garni, which is a mix of herbs used to simmer in stews and sauces. The heavy essential oil of thyme holds up well when simmering or baking. The fresh camphor-like flavor is a nice addition to vinegar and oil blends. My favorite cooking variety is lemon thyme: Mix fresh sprigs with olive oil, spread the olive oil/thyme mix over

Lemon Thyme
(Thymus x citriodorus)

Variegated broad leaf Thyme
(Thymus pulegioides 'Foxley')

chicken or fish just before placing in the oven to bake or broil. Place fresh sprigs on fish and chicken. Add to bread dough and lemon cake desserts to infuse a unique aroma and flavor to baked goods. (For recipes that use thyme, see pages 99, 104, 107, 108, 110, 112, 113, 135 and 164.)

OTHER USES: Use a strong thyme infusion in water as a gargle to soothe a sore throat. Infuse thyme in natural witch hazel to create a refreshing, healing skin wash.

MAKE YOUR OWN
herb "garnish bouquet"
(known in the culinary world as bouquet garni)

Popular in French cooking, these are tiny fresh
herb bouquets tied with cooking twine and floated in
simmering soups and stews. Sometimes the herbs are
wrapped in cheesecloth and tied to make them easy to
remove from the pot (bouquet garni is removed before
serving). In Julia Child's *Mastering the Art of French
Cooking*, her famous Boeuf Bourguignon recipe calls
for an herb bouquet made of 4 sprigs parsley,
2 sprigs thyme and 1 bay leaf.

TWO

Unusual or Tender Herbs

Four that you should know about

What are unusual or tender herbs? These are herbs that are not commonly grown in every herb garden but are definitely worth a try. Some are tender to climates with hard winters and so can be treated as annuals. If you're feeling adventurous, try growing some in the garden. They are good additions for unusual flavors in your spice and seasoning cabinet.

LEMON GRASS: *Cymbopogon citratus* is a tall, grass-like perennial. It can be grown as an annual in a pot in areas with long, warm summers, but will not tolerate a frost. Most Asian markets will have fresh leaves that can be rooted in water; they will produce roots fast and can be planted in soil in a pot within a month. Use the tender young leaves whole, swirl them in simmering soups during cooking and remove before serving. The white base of the plants is where the best flavor is. Chop up and use to add a light lemony flavor to mild dishes and white sauces. Sprinkle on white fish and chicken. For a sweet, citrusy refresher, make a simple sugar syrup flavored with lemon grass to add to sparkling water, then garnish with lemon slices.

BAY LEAVES: Bay laurel *(Laurus nobilis)*, also known as sweet bay, is a large, shrubby evergreen native to Mediterranean climate regions of the world. It is hardy outside to USDA zones 8 and above. The leaves have a spicy fragrance when crushed. Use fresh leaves for a sweeter flavor. Dried leaves will be less pungent but will have a more pronounced camphor-like aroma. Bay leaves are typically used in pickling spices, soups, stews, roasting meats and as flavoring for vinegars. Because the leaf is very tough and does not disintegrate in cooking, it is one of the few herbs that can be added early in simmering and cooking. A note of caution: Always remove whole bay leaves from a dish before serving, the leaves are hard to digest and can cause choking.

STEVIA: Stevia *(Stevia rebaudiana)* is grown as an annual in USDA zones under 9. With the popularity of stevia, new cultivars from seed like *Stevia rebaudiana* 'Candy' are available for sale from specialty herb seed suppliers (see Resources). The very sweet leaves have the substance "stevioside," which is said to be two to three hundred times sweeter than sucrose. Leaves can be harvested anytime, but will be at their sweetest just before the plant flowers. Leaves can be used fresh or dried. Crumble the leaves in tea blends to add natural sweetness. Add to creamy fruit sauces, marinades and yogurt. Because the leaves do not dissolve or break down easily, they are not good to use in baking.

SAFFRON: The treasured delicate spice is taken from the dried stigmas of the fall-flowering crocus. The plant is a bulb *(Crocus sativus)* that flowers a light lilac color with deep, dark-reddish stigmas, Because of its tiny threads it must be picked by hand and handled carefully. It takes about 225,000 stigmas to make up a pound of saffron, making it one of the most expensive spices for purchase. Saffron is used very lightly; too much and it will add a bitter flavor. The stigma will impart a deep color into liquids and light-colored sauces and sides such as rice. Grow your own crocus and harvest the stigmas carefully, drying them on screens; or purchase only brightly-colored threads. Broken stigmas or powder quickly lose their distinct flavor.

Complements: Other Flavorful Plants

Taste-mates from beyond the herb garden

What do I mean by plants that are complements? These are the spices, fruits, vegetables and edible flowers that add variety for seasoning mixes and flavor infusions. They complement the herb recipes and give diversity to blending seasonings.

IS IT AN **HERB** OR A **SPICE?**

Both herbs and spices are the flavor makers in recipes, but are they the same?

Typically, herbs are the green parts of the plants, like the leaves (basil and mint) and stems (chives). Generally soft-stemmed and herbaceous, and not woody like trees.

Herbs are represented in the annual, perennial, biennial families. They have distinctive essential oils in their soft plant tissues; it is what gives them their flavor and fragrance.

Spices are generally classified as the woody textures of aromatic bark (cinnamon), seeds and pods (cloves, allspice and star anise) of plants that are grown in warm, temperate climates of the world.

There is one plant that is both an herb and a spice. The leaf of the plant cilantro (*Corinadrum sativum*) is an herb used for its distinct flavor, while the seed from the plant is the spice known as coriander.

SPICES:

- **ALLSPICE:** Allspice is one of the few spices grown in the Western Hemisphere. The *Pimenta* species of trees are found in Jamaica, Mexico and Central America. The dried ripe fruit has a flavor similar to a mix of cloves, nutmeg and cinnamon, hence the name allspice. Commonly used in spiced beverages, pickling and to flavor fruit desserts. The powdered form can be used measure-for-measure as a substitute for nutmeg or cloves.

- **ANISE:** *Pimpinella anisum* is an annual plant. It needs long, hot summer weather to ripen the seeds properly. The dried seeds (which are technically the fruits of the plant) have a strong, sweet, licorice flavor when eaten. The flavor will infuse through bread and cookie doughs and add a unique flavor to teas.

- **CINNAMON:** A valued spice for centuries, cinnamon is the dried inner the bark of the *Cinnamomum* species of trees. Stick cinnamon is used to flavor hot beverages like tea or hot chocolate. Whole sticks are added when cooking or pickling fruits. The warming aroma of powdered cinnamon enhances the flavor of dessert dishes and savory meat meals.

- **CLOVES:** Cloves are the dried, unopen flower bud from the clove tree (*Syzygium* sp.), a plant native to the East Indies. The trees bear successive blooms all through the year, producing abundant crops of buds to harvest. Cloves are used whole or ground and are popular in dessert mixes. The whole cloves are also used as a seasoning when canning relishes, chutneys and spiced pickled fruits.

- **CUMIN:** Cumin is the seed of the plant *Cuminum cyminum*. Cumin has a strong, earthy flavor typically used in powdered form. It is popular in ethnic dishes, curry mixes, chili powders and enhances tomatoes and avocados in salsa and guacamole blends.

- **GINGER:** The dried and peeled rhizome of a tropical plant, *Zingiber officinale*, ginger is a warming spice used in blends for desserts and savory dishes. Good quality ginger powder should be a deep beige color with a pungent aroma. It will have a sweet, hot taste that lingers on the tongue. Whole ginger root can be grated for use to add a pungent warming flavor to liquids.

- **PEPPER:** Pepper, the spice, not the vegetable, is one of the most popular and common spices used in cooking. It is a berry from a perennial vine, *Piper nigrum*, native to the East Indies and grown in warm regions of the world. Black pepper is the berry picked underripe and dried; it is the spiciest form of the berry when dried. White pepper is picked when in a riper stage; after drying, the outer hull is removed. Colored peppercorns are all taken from the same plant – they are just picked at varying stages of maturity. Note: Pink peppercorns are not true peppercorns, but a softer, milder berry from the Brazilian pepper tree *(Schinus terebinthifolia)*. Grind or crush whole peppercorns when adding to sauces or recipes. Use white pepper when you don't want the black flecks to appear in light or white sauces.

- **MUSTARD SEED:** Dry mustard powders are typically a blend of numerous species of mustards. The blending of different ones lends characters of flavor to each mustard. The hottest spice from mustard is from the portion of the seed just under the hull.

- **STAR ANISE:** Differing from anise "seed" listed above, star anise is the unique-shaped seed pod of an evergreen tree, *Illicium verum*. The seeds contained in the points of the star are ground for use in cooking. Star anise has a sweet licorice and warming aroma. It is a hard, woody seed pod used with other woody spices in mulled wine and cider. Star anise is best known as one of the spices in Chinese Five Spice powder, a spicy blend of cinnamon, cloves, fennel, star anise and peppercorns.

● **VANILLA BEANS:** *Vanilla planifiola* is an orchid that produces a long seed pod. The cured seed pods when split open are filled with tiny black seeds. Use whole beans by splitting them open and scraping the insides for blending into sauces, creams and liquids. Alcohol extracts the flavoring from vanilla "beans".

Make your own vanilla extract: You need 3 whole vanilla beans to about 8 ounces of vodka. Carefully split the vanilla beans open. Put the beans in a clean glass bottle (cut them up if needed to make them fit in the jar). Pour vodka over the beans until they are covered. Cover the bottle tightly and shake well. Allow the mix to steep for about a month; shake occasionally to stir up any seeds and residue that have settled to the bottom. The extract is ready when you smell a strong scent of vanilla and less of the vodka. Leave the beans in the bottle. After using some and the bottle is about ½ to ⅓ empty, top with vodka again and allow to steep for a few weeks. The same beans will continue to flavor the extract for another full recipe.

VEGETABLES, FRUIT AND ROOTS

- **CITRUS, LEMON, LIME, ORANGE:** The peels of citrus are the thin outer rind of mature fruits. Immature or unripe citrus peel will tend to be more bitter. When peeling rind, slice thinly and avoid the white, spongy pith. Use peels to add texture and a note of citrus to baked goods and rice dishes. The dried peels can be chopped or crushed and added to teas and dry mixes. To add a strong flavor of citrus juice to a dry mix, crystalized lemon and lime is available for purchase (see Resources).

- **GARLIC:** A pungent member of the allium family, garlic is a bulb that is easily grown in the garden. Plant bulbs early in the year and harvest in late summer or fall. Use whole cloves or chop for use in liquids. Garlic is available in dried, dehydrated and powder for adding to dry seasoning mixes. Don't be fooled by a weak-smelling powder. In its dehydrated form it doesn't smell as strong, but when added to moisture it will rehydrate back to its powerful pungency. About 1/8 teaspoon of garlic powder equals an average-size garlic clove.

- **HORSERADISH:** A hardy plant, horseradish is a white root popular for its hot, strong flavor. The roots have better flavor when harvested after the first heavy frost in the fall. Dehydrated horseradish is available at spice markets, but use this form cautiously; it may smell mild in the jar, but once rehydrated it will trigger an enzyme activity that will bring it back to its powerful pungency.

- **ONIONS:** Onions can be used fresh from the garden, but readily available forms of dehydrated onions, both powder and chopped, make them easy to add to blends and mixes. The process of preserving doesn't typically lessen the pungency and flavor of onions.

- **PEPPERS:** The *Capsicum* species is a large variety of plants that produce hot, sweet and spicy fruits. In cooking and seasoning, the chilies vary in levels of heat and tastes, based on what cultivar they are – from mild and sweet (bell peppers) to tongue-scorching heat (Habanero). Dried, crushed chilies make cayenne pepper and paprika. Grow your own peppers to dry or purchase in flake and powder form.

EDIBLE FLOWERS

Edible flowers are a nice accent to herb seasoning and blends by adding flavor and color. Get to know more about edible flowers and the parts to eat. Some flowers have delicious petals while other parts may be bitter. Here are a few uses in recipes throughout the book.

- **CALENDULA:** The golden petals of calendula can be added fresh to salads to impart a slightly bitter zing. Use dried petals as a garnish on butter and cream cheese. To use, harvest the flower head whole and dry on flat screens. After the flower head is completely dry, gently pull the petals away from the flower head and store in a glass jar.

ELDERFLOWER: A common large shrub, elderberry *(Sambucus* spp.) produces creamy, white flowers in the early summer and deep purple berries in late summer. The honey-scented flowers are short lived, so when the season is on, preserve them into sugar syrup for later use in cocktails and to liven up sparkling water. Decorate cakes with the flowers and top with a glaze made from elderflower cordial and confectioner's sugar. The berries add color and flavor to jams and pies. Serve elderberry cordial after dinner or as a hot toddy to soothe a sore throat.

MARIGOLD: This is the common garden flower *Tagetes*, but for the best flavor and edibility, be picky about the cultivars you grow for food. The varieties Lemon Gem and Tangerine Gem *(Tagetes tenuifolia)* are two that have a citrus aroma and flavor. Snip the flower heads and put them in green salads and on sandwiches. Freeze the flowers whole into ice cubes to use in iced teas.

NASTURTIUMS: This easy-to-grow annual produces vibrant, large flowers and rounded leaves. Both have a peppery taste. Use the leaves in place of lettuce on sandwiches and in green salad mixes. Fill the flower heads with herbed cream cheese for a delicate summer hors d'oeuvre.

BORAGE: The blue flowers of borage have a mild aroma and taste of cucumbers. Use them fresh to garnish salad, butters and soft cheeses. Candy them (see recipe on next page for candied violets) to use as edible décor on cupcakes. Freeze the flowers into ice cubes for flowery garnish to lemonade and cocktails. The flowers do not dry well, so use them in season. To harvest: Cut the flower heads off the plant. Hold the dark center of the flower and gently pull the flower to detach it away from the calyx (base of the stem, where the sepals attach to the flower).

- **VIOLAS:** The best fresh wintergreen-like flavor is in the spreading perennial *Viola cornuta* and the more common Johnny-jump-ups *(Viola tricolor)*. Colorful and sweet, violas can be used to decorate cakes and muffins. Use them in fresh green or fruit salads. Preserve them by freezing them into ice cubes.

CANDIED VIOLAS FOR GARNISH ON DESSERTS:

1 egg white, beaten until frothy
1 cup extra-fine sugar
Fresh, unblemished violas

Using a fine, small paintbrush, paint all sides of the flowers with egg white, dust with sugar and allow to air dry completely on a flat, parchment-covered surface.

- **ROSES:** The petals of fragrant shrub and rugosa roses are edible and add beautiful color to tea blends and salt mixes. Strongly fragrant roses are the most important factor in using roses for culinary dishes. The fragrance means the essential oil is strong and so will be the flavor. Harvest roses just as they open. Remove the petals from the center and cut off the white bitter base of each petal. Place on drying screens in a single layer. Once completely dry, store whole in a glass jar. Fresh petals can be sugared and used as a garnish on desserts, butters and creamy cheeses. Create a floral drink blended with rosewater and champagne; float petals in the glass and give a toast.

FOUR

Harvest & Preserve Your Herbal Bounty

For maximum flavor – fresh, dried or frozen

Harvest herbs through the growing season for fresh use. Many herbs exhibit their best character and essence when used fresh. There are also numerous herbs that dry well and add their distinguishing taste to grilling rubs, seasoning salts, teas and dried blends. The overall goal in any harvesting method is to quickly preserve the volatile essential oil in the plants.

In the garden, herb harvesting is an ongoing task. Cutting most leafy perennial herbs through the season encourages a flush of new growth to keep the flavor coming. Annual herbs with enough warm weather left will also reward you with leafy abundance when cut regularly.

THE OPTIMUM TIME TO HARVEST

It really depends on the individual herb and on what part you need to harvest: leaf, flower, stem or seed. Each plant has its moment where it is best picked for flavor. Sometimes it is when the leaves are tender and new and sometimes it is at a late flowering stage. Being familiar with the herb, the growing stage of the season and observing the garden will signal when you need to harvest. To discover the best of tips for an individual herb, consult the herb profile section in this book, Chapter One.

BEYOND FRESH HERBS: DRYING AND FREEZING

It's not just about using fresh herbs in the moment. You can save herbs to use in seasoning recipes and mixes, giving you flavor throughout the year. When should you harvest for drying or freezing? When plants have a leafy abundance or when the end of the growing season is near.

GOOD TO KNOW:

- Cut herbs and immediately take the next step to preparing them for drying or freezing. Don't leave heaps of them waiting around until you have time to get to them.

- Dry the parts of the plant needed in their whole form (unless noted). When you cut, tear or break the plant it releases the essential oils, thus releasing (losing) flavor and aroma. If you're drying or freezing for later use, you don't want to lose any of those essential oils prematurely.

- Process only as much as you can deal with at one time. The faster you can get an herb dried the better the color and flavor.

HARVEST AND PRESERVATION GLOSSARY

ANNUAL HERBS: Cut annual herbs through the growing season as needed for fresh use. Leave about 4 to 5 inches of leafy growth on the plant to flush out more leaves for future harvesting. At the end of the individual plant's growing season or when frost threatens, cut the entire plant. Strip off any dead or faded leaves. Dry or freeze to preserve.

BUNDLE (HOW-TO): Bundling herbs with strong stems allows you to easily hang them to dry. Gather a small bunch of stems. Strip the lower leaves off the bundle and bind tightly with a rubber band. It is best to keep bundles small; bulky, tight, large bundles will not dry well and are susceptible to mold and rot.

CLEANING: As you are cutting herbs, lightly shake them to dislodge any bugs or remove excess moisture. Plants must be completely bug-free and clean before preserving or to use in cooking. If you are planning an herb harvest, consider watering the plants in the garden the day before and showering the leaves well to clean them and remove bugs. Do not wash them with water after cutting them; instead, lightly rinse if needed and gently pat dry. Avoid any damage or breakage that will release the essential oils from the plant.

CUTTING: When gathering herbs from the garden, use sharp, clean tools. Take a flat gathering basket to transport herbs as you are snipping them. Work quickly and keep cut herbs out of the hot sun. The longer they are exposed to air or heat, the more the flavor and aromas will dissipate.

DRYING RACKS: To dry bundles well, you need a place to hang them up. One of my favorite racks to use is a wood dowel laundry rack. The racks fold flat for storage and when it's harvest time, I set up the rack and hang multiple bundles at a time. You can also get creative and repurpose hanging racks used for pots and pans or an old metal frame of a lampshade to hang your herb bundles on.

DRYING SCREENS: These are flat mesh screens used for drying delicate herbs, flowers and seeds. Place gathered herb parts in a single layer on the screen. The mesh allows air circulation all around the plants. Place screens on the flat top of wood dowel laundry racks or on a flat surface propped up a few inches with blocks to keep air circulating under the racks. To keep dust from settling on the plants, rest a paper towel over the herbs on the top of the screen.

FLOWERS: Harvest the flowers of herbs just before or when they open up in full petal. If color begins to fade then so does flavor and aroma, so timing is important. It is best to cut individual flower heads and dry them flat on screens. When growing herbs for seasoning, like basil and oregano, don't allow the plants to flower. Otherwise much of the flavor will be lost to the flowers.

FREEZING HERBS: Some herbs do well in the freezer. Generally, the heavier texture the plant, like mint, oregano and rosemary, the better it will freeze. Delicate herbs tend to turn to an unrecognizable mush during the freezing process. Frozen herbs do not hold their shape and will be a bit ugly because the freezing process breaks down their plant cells – but the flavor will still be retained. Frozen herbs can be melted into simmering dishes, soups, stews, sauces and other liquids. The easiest way to freeze plants is the ice cube method:

● In an ice cube tray, fill each space of the tray with herb leaves. Cut or tear them as needed to fit in the spaces. Top the spaces with water, making sure all of the herb is submerged. Place the tray in the freezer until solid. Once frozen, the cubes can be stored in a zip-close freezer bag.

BAKING SHEET METHOD: Large, sturdy leaves like sage or the stems of chives can be chopped and placed on a flat baking sheet. Scatter leaves or stems in a single layer to avoid clumping. Place the baking sheet in the freezer. Allow to freeze about 4 hours or overnight. Place the frozen herbs in a freezer-safe glass canning jar and seal well. The herbs can be easily measured and used in sauces, soups and warm dishes for fresh garden flavor any time of year.

FRESH, BOUQUET-STYLE: Fresh-cut herbs can be stored in a vase with water to keep them fresh for up to a week. Fill a clean glass vase (a wide-mouth glass canning jar is perfect) with fresh water. Cut a bunch of herbs. Strip the lower leaves from the stems so there will not be leaves under water. Place the "bouquet" in the jar of water and store in the refrigerator. Fresh leaves can be harvested when needed.

HANG DRY: The easiest method to dry herbs. Choose a place to hang herbs that is cool, dark and well ventilated. In a stuffy area or times of high humidity, run a fan to circulate air around the plants to help them dry quickly. Avoid any sources of heat. The amount of time needed to hang dry varies by the size of the bundle, thickness of the plants and how much moisture content they have.

LEAVES: Harvest leaves individually or on whole stems. Through the growing season, new leaves are the most flavorful. For drying, keep the leaves whole. Cut, tear or crush them just before use in recipes.

PAPER BAG METHOD: To keep bundles dust-free during the drying process cover them with a paper bag. Bundle herbs as described earlier. Place a paper bag over the bundle and tie with garden twine, tightly around the end (where you placed the rubber band hold the herb bundle together). Hang the bag from the string in your drying area. This works especially well for herbs that shatter easily, like lavender buds; the drying buds will drop in the bottom of the bag instead of all over the floor. Mesh produce drawstring bags are a great reusable bag to also use for this method.

PERENNIAL HERBS: Most perennial herbs can be cut leaving about 4 to 6 inches or a third of the plant above ground, to encourage new, fresh growth for repicking. Many plants will produce enough for another crop for continuous cutting. Try to cut plants attractively in order to keep a nice shape for the season. Herbaceous herbs that die to the ground in winter can be harvested completely at the end of their growing season. *Tip:* Do not cut into the wood on herbs like rosemary, lavender or sage in the late season before the onset of winter or prior to hard frosts. Cutting severely will make them vulnerable to winter damage.

QUANTITY: In growing season, pick only as much as you need or can process at a time. The plants are much better left growing as long as they are not over-aging or threatened by frost damage.

SHELF LIFE: The shelf life of herbs depends on the individual plant and how it is harvested and preserved. Fresh bouquet-style herbs can last up to a week if refrigerated. The shelf life of dry herbs is harvest-to-harvest. Try to use herbs within a year. Toss or compost them once you have another crop, in season, to cut. Frozen herbs should be used within 6 to 12 months.

STORAGE: Glass jars. Store dried herbs in tightly sealed glass jars – cleaned and sterilized. (See page 96 for how to sterilize and clean jars.) Glass is best for retaining flavor. Since most herbs look alike after they dry, be sure to label the jars. Store jars in a dark cabinet, away from heat and light.

SEEDS: The seed or pod must be picked at the proper time. The seeds can ripen quickly as the season progresses. You may need to check the seedpods daily before they open and spill seeds onto the garden. The seeds need to be ripe and no longer green, but before they fall to the ground and disperse. Dry the seeds flat on drying screens. When seeds cling to sturdy seedpods or umbel flowers like dill, hang them to dry completely by using the paper bag method. When the herbs are dry in the paper bag, shake the bag to thresh the seeds from the plants. The seeds will gather at the bottom of the bag to be easily poured out into a glass storage jar or tin.

STORAGE: Metal tins. Clean metal tins can be used for dry herbs, mixes and teas. (See page 96 for how to clean tins.) Be sure to label the tins. Store in a dark cabinet, away from heat and light.

TIMING YOUR HARVEST: Generally, the best time of day to harvest for optimum flavor is in the morning after the dew dries off the plants. This is the point where the essential oils in the plants typically are the heaviest, before the heat of the day starts to release the aroma of the herbs into the air.

TOOLS: Use clean, sharp scissors or pruners to cut the plants. Never pull or tug at the stems or flowers or you might damage or loosen the roots of the plant. A few of my favorite cutting tools include:

- **Grape scissors:** Their small blades let you easily snip single stems without damaging surrounding ones.
- **Regular garden pruners:** These are good for tough, woody stems like rosemary.
- **Scissors:** A good, sharp pair of inexpensive scissors are usually my go-to for when I grab a handful of thinner stems like lavender or chives. Save one good pair for herb cutting only (not ones you use for fabric). Clean your cutting tools with kitchen disinfecting wipes to remove plant remnants and oily residue after harvesting.

PART TWO

Create!

FIVE

Working with Herbs in the Kitchen

Get ready, get set…!

I love to mix and play with plant materials that give flavor from the garden. The herbs I grow and a few staples from my pantry are all I need to create seasoning mixes, dressings, flavored vinegars and so much more. I am an experimenter. A little of this, a little of that, and a pinch of pungency. You know…that kind of cook.

Sometimes my experiment turns out amazing and I wish I could remember how much of something I used, and sometimes I fail miserably on the flavor. (I could tell you stories that involve too much rosemary or cilantro!)

Putting together recipes for this book has been fun and flavorful – testing and re-testing, ever alert to the play of the herbal flavor notes. And, of course, making sure my measurements are correct for you to try. It has been a very fragrant kitchen! Most of the recipes have been ones I have used for many years and have scribbled on tattered pieces of paper or taught in one of my herb workshops, or have been rummaged out of my memory. There are also many new concoctions just for this book.

What I'd really like you to know is most of these are starting points to seasoning. Think of these recipes as base notes to your culinary flavor adventures. Let your taste buds guide you to explore more. For example, if you love garlic, then add a little more to a recipe that calls for it. As you get more into creating your own herbal concoctions don't go crazy with too many different herbs or spices that are not in the recipe already. Just add more of a particular herb that is already listed. A good rule of thumb is to add another ¼ of a measure and then do a taste test.

Just remember: Herbs in cooking are meant to enhance not overpower, so use in moderation. Become familiar with the taste of the herbs you'll be using. Sage, thyme, rosemary and oregano, for instance, are strong-flavored, so you'll want to go lightly and adjust to your taste buds.

When do I add herbs during cooking? Add most herbs to recipes 30 minutes before the end of cooking time (unless directed otherwise) and simmer slowly to release their flavorful oils. Exception: Some of the lighter-flavored herbs should be added at the end of cooking time so the flavor is not lost to the heat of cooking.

Some of the recipes here are "Basic" or "Any-Herb" recipes. These are ones you can really have fun with. Start with one variety of herb that you have an abundance of and try it. You may have to adjust to your taste. The Basic Herb Butter recipe on page 151 is one of the easiest to start with: Make a flavored butter and try it on a plain cracker

WHAT'S COOKING?

Here are some classic herb/food pairings, but always let your taste buds be your guide:

With beef try: Rosemary, Chives, Marjoram

With poultry try: Oregano, Garlic, Rosemary

With fish try: Dill, Lemon thyme

With fruit try: Mint, Lavender, Rose geranium

With soups try: Parsley, Basil, Dill, Oregano

With salads try: Chives, French tarragon, Parsley, Basil

With infused water try: Lemon verbena, Lavender, Parsley

to see how the herb mingles in the base of butter. It simply becomes a flavorful herb in a spreadable form. Remember to also let the ingredients blend and marry together, sometimes overnight. As essential oils from the plants are released into oil, salt and other base ingredients (like butter), they will become more refined and flavorful the longer they sit. After the mix has rested, taste again and add more if needed.

SOME GENERAL RULES FOR HERB RECIPES:

Take care to notice if the recipe calls for dry or fresh herbs. Sometimes they can be used interchangeably, but sometimes the difference in moisture content can alter the flavor outcome.

Many of the recipes are small batches and can be doubled for gift giving or to provide a good stock for the spice cabinet, especially for when the fresh herbs are out of season.

USE DRIED HERBS WITH:
dry base elements like sugar or salt

USE FRESH HERBS IF POSSIBLE WITH:
liquid bases like oils, vinegar or water

BOOST YOUR FLAVOR

- *Flavor and aroma are connected:* Things that smell good taste good. Make sure mixes have appetizing aromas. You will see notes throughout the recipes on testing the readiness of a blend by its fragrance.

- *Colors and arrangement of seasoning mixes are important:* Make a feast for the eyes. How a mix looks will broadcast how enticing it will be when mixed in a main dish. This is a good reason to harvest properly.

- *Texture (crunchy, chewy, creamy):* It's no secret that food is better when it is palatable. You can make a difference in a successful herb blend with the use of fine or coarse grinds, and how well things are mixed together.

- *A delicate balance:* A recipe should have just enough spiciness to flavor but not overpower the main ingredient it is seasoning. Example: Sweetness is added to entice the taste buds, but not make the mouth water too much.

- **Measuring for dried or fresh herbs:** When a recipe calls for dried herbs and you'd like to use fresh, triple the measure. (Example: If a recipe calls for 1 teaspoon of dried basil, use 3 teaspoons of fresh.)

- **Measuring for other ingredients:** For dry ingredients use a dry measuring cup. For liquids use a glass liquid measuring cup; place it on a flat work surface and pour in the ingredient to the specified line of measure.

- **Washing fresh herbs:** Gently rinse fresh herbs and spin or pat dry just before using in a recipe. When cleaning, you do not want to break fresh plants too much or wash the flavor down the drain.

- **Allowing time for flavors to blend:** In most uncooked foods, like fruit recipes and salad dressings, the herb flavors need to marry; add them and allow time for the mix to set before serving.

- **Going easy on herb combinations:** If you are experimenting with a new dish using herbs, don't combine too many at once. Allow each individual herb to make a statement.

- **Eliminating salt from your diet?** Remove the salt from the recipe and add more of the herb used in the dish to pump up the flavor, minus the salt. A good starting point is to add another ¼ of the original measure of herb. Then add more herb to taste.

- **A note about clumping:** Because most dry mixes do not have anti-caking agents, mixes might clump in storage. Before use, give them a good shake to loosen them or put the mix in a plastic zip-close bag and pound with a rolling pin or the back of a wooden spoon to break it up. It also helps to store tightly sealed jars upside down.

UTENSIL GLOSSARY

BAMBOO SKEWERS: Use to stir mixes. They can be used and thrown away if herb flavors and coatings get on them.

CHEESECLOTH: A loosely woven, gauzy fabric. Use for straining herbs out of liquids. The fabric can be easily placed to form over odd-size bottle openings. Also, good for bundling herb mixes to simmer in sauces, soups and to make tea.

GRINDER: Use a coffee bean grinder or spice grinder to process dried herbs into a powdered form. Tip to clean your grinder: add ¼ cup uncooked rice and pulse the grinder. Pour out the rice and then wipe the grinder with a soft cloth that has been dampened with vodka. The rice will help absorb and remove any remnants and the vodka will remove oily residue.

HERB SCISSORS: A pair of scissors with multiple blades that minces herbs easily and cleanly.

MESH KITCHEN SINK STRAINER: These are a handy size that fits the top of canning jars. Use to get rid of herbs from vinegars, wines and other liquids where the plants need to be removed.

MORTAR AND PESTLE: A two-piece kitchen tool used for crushing and grinding dry herbs together, or chunky ingredients, to make them into a paste. This is a good tool to use when a spice grinder is too powerful. A mortar and pestle can leave larger colorful bits of herbs and spices, while a spice grinder can quickly turn a mix to powder. Choose your tool based on what kind of consistency you want your dried mix to be.

MUDDLER: A tool made of metal or wood that is essential for crushing herbs and larger ingredients into liquids. Popular tool for bartenders to smash flavor ingredients into cocktails.

WOODEN SPOONS: Handy for stirring and pressing herbs into liquids. Many herbs have a chemical reaction to metal utensils, and can turn herbs a dark, unappealing color. Use wooden spoons and bamboo skewers (as noted above) to avoid discoloration.

PREPARATION TERMS TO KNOW

BRUISE: To bruise herbs into a mix means to push on them or slightly crush them to help release the essential oils into the mix. You are not mincing or breaking the herbs down too much, just enough to release flavor and aroma.

CHOP: Place whole fresh herbs in a tidy stack on a cutting board and slice using a rocking motion with a sharp knife. Chop the herbs, crisscrossing the knife until they are the size of pieces desired.

GARNISH: An item used to decorate food.

INFUSION: The process of taking an herb from your garden and making it into a pourable liquid form. Spices, fruits and vegetables can also be used to add flavoring to the liquid. You start with a base liquid: water, oil, vinegar, wine, liquor. The flavor of the ingredients is put into the base and allowed to steep. Steeping can be by heat, cold or room temperature based on the plant and what it is mixed with. The "base" ingredients can then be used to introduce the flavor into another a culinary dish without having the leafy or woody pieces from the plants. Other infusions will add variety to cooking, like a sweet flavoring from honey or the tartness of vinegar. Infused liquors and wines add refreshing herbal flavoring to cocktails.

MINCE: To chop or cut into small fine pieces.

POULTICE: Large pieces of herbs, crushed together with a liquid (usually water or oil) to create a moist mass of plant material.

STRIP: Describes the process of removing leaves from a stem or woody branch.

UNBLEACHED MUSLIN: A 100% cotton fabric with a tight weave. Place the fabric over the top of a jar or bottle and pour the liquid through to filter herb pieces out of the liquid. Small drawstring muslin bags can be used to hold herbs, spices and tea mixes during cooking.

STORAGE AND PACKAGING: Use clean sterilized jars for storage and finished packaging. Glass is best for the herbs to

retain the best flavor. To sterilize jars, wash and scrub away dust and debris in hot soapy water. Rinse well and dry. Place empty jars in a pot of boiling water. The pot needs to be large enough to completely submerge the jars into the water. Bring water to a full boil and continue to boil for the jars for 15 minutes. Allow to cool slightly and remove jars from pan and air dry.

Metal tins can be used for dry herbs, mixes and teas. Wash the tins in hot, soapy water. Allow to air dry. Wipe the inside with a paper towel soaked in vodka to remove any oily residue. Allow to dry completely before use. Always label your jars and tins. Many herbs look alike after they are dried. Use a glass marking pen to write on the outside of jars.

SIX

Dry Seasoning Mixes

Your go-to blends for everyday seasoning

These are the mixes you will store in your pantry in a convenient ready-to-use form. Keep them handy for adding your herb garden flavors to cooking all year long. I love that these are multi-use too. Shake them on a fresh leafy salad or flavor up a marinade for grilling meats. Stir them into olive oil to add zing to fresh tossed pasta. Store your dried mixes in a tightly sealed glass jar in a cabinet away from heat or light. Most mixes will keep for 6 months to a year.

ANY-HERB SALT

As the recipe name suggests, you can use any herb you have in the garden. Simple to make. Herb salts can be used as a base for other seasoning mixes or straight from the bottle to season and flavor vegetables, meats and other savory dishes. Because salt acts as a natural preservative this recipe can also be used to capture the flavor of fresh herbs like tarragon that don't hold their flavor well through the drying process.

HERB SALT MEASURING RATIO:

4 parts minced fresh or dry herbs
1 part medium-grind sea salt

PREPARATION:

Combine the herbs and the salt and lightly crush the mix in a mortar and pestle. Stir until it is well mixed. Add the salt mix to a glass jar and cover tightly. Shake before use. Mixes made with fresh herbs may clump and need to be stirred occasionally and should be used within 4 to 6 weeks. Mixes made with dried herbs will have a shelf life of up to a year or more.

NO-SALT HERB BLEND

When using the right combination of herbs in dry blends you hardly miss the salt. Pungent herbs complemented with lemon and garlic tingle the taste buds just as well as salt can. Use this blend to sprinkle on salads and to season meats for grilling. All herb ingredients are used in dried form.

INGREDIENTS:

2 tablespoons dried thyme

2 tablespoons dried oregano

1 teaspoon dried rosemary

1 teaspoon dehydrated garlic granules

2 teaspoons crystalized lemon powder

1 teaspoon dried lemon peel, chopped fine

Dash of ground black pepper

PREPARATION:

Mix all ingredients well, then slightly crush them in a mortar with a pestle to break them down. This mix can be ground to a finer powder in a grinder. Store in a glass jar with a shaker top. Keep jar tightly sealed to avoid clumping.

Recipe to try:

HEALTHY EGG-FREE SALAD DRESSING

INGREDIENTS:

½ cup light olive oil

½ cup unsweetened coconut milk (full fat)

3 tablespoons apple cider vinegar

1 tablespoon No-Salt Herb Blend

PREPARATION:

Whip together all ingredients well until smooth and creamy. This mix gets better the longer the herbs combine with the other base ingredients. Refrigerate for 3 to 4 hours or overnight before serving.

WHICH SALT?

COARSE SALT: Coarse refers to the size and grind of different salts. These are large pieces of salt and are used in grinders for a fresh ground salt flavor. Coarse salts will have a longer shelf life because they are less moisture sensitive. Use this size of salt in herb salt blends. A more flavorful salt is created when you are able to grind the salt and herbs to break them down together. This will release the essence of the herbs into the salt.

FINISHING AND FLAKE SALTS: These salts have textures that are used to make a nice presentation to a dish right before serving. The larger flakes add texture and crunch. They also dissolve quickly in the mouth, adding a fresh salt taste that will not overpower when used in the right ratio with other herbs and spices.

FLAVORED SALTS: Smoked or wine-infused sea salt crystals are used to add another layer of flavor to herb mixes. (Choose smoked salts that have been flavored by natural smoke methods and not by using a liquid smoke.) Flavored salts are best used with strong herbs like rosemary, sage, oregano and savory.

FRENCH GREY SEA SALT: A moist textured salt. French sea salt, or sel gris, are hand harvested sea salts. They are unrefined so the salt retains trace minerals from seawater. French grey salt is good to use with delicate herbs like lemon verbena, roses and dill.

HAWAIIAN SEA SALT: Authentic Hawaiian sea salts are hand harvested and are colorful because of the clay stirred up in the harvesting process. The deep color of red salt has a mellow, earthy flavor from the red clay. Black sea salt is bound with activated black charcoal, giving it a shiny black look that adds color to herbal salt mixes.

HIMALAYAN SALT: Hand mined from ancient sea salt deposits. Himalayan salt is typically a deep pink color or a muted mix of pinks. It is said that this salt is one of the purest salts available and is heavy with trace minerals. Because of its unadulterated quality Himalayan salt is popular in skin care and spa treatments. This salt can be used in any recipe calling for sea salt.

KOSHER SALT: Labeled kosher salt is referring to a flake salt use in the preparation of meat in Jewish dietary guidelines. It has a clean, fresh taste that dissolves easily with liquid or on the tongue. This is the classic chunky salt used on pretzels. Another type of kosher salt is a regular grind salt that has been processed to meet kosher certifications outlined by Jewish law.

SEA SALT: This has become a generic term encompassing unrefined salt harvested from a living ocean or sea. Because it is less processed, most sea salts retain trace minerals found in the parts of the world they have been harvested from. It has become

popular because it has a pure, clean flavor that doesn't overpower herbs when used in seasoning mixes or cooking.

TABLE SALT: The most common salt available, it is typically harvested from salt mines. It is refined to the point that is it almost pure sodium chloride with little or no trace minerals. The refining process makes it have a more bitter taste that comes through strong in cooking and is used for brining. Do not use this stronger salt in seasoning mixes because it may overpower and throw off the balance of all the other flavors.

LAVENDER FRENCH GREY SEL ET POIVRE
(SALT AND PEPPER)

The lavender buds give just enough of an earthy flavor to the salt without overpowering it. Swap this blend for your daily table salt to kick up the flavor of any dish you would normally use salt and pepper on.

INGREDIENTS:

1 tablespoon dried lavender buds
3 tablespoons coarse grind French grey sea salt
Ground black peppercorns to taste
  (approximately ½ teaspoon)

PREPARATION:

Mix the lavender buds and salt together. Lightly crush together to break down and infuse the lavender flavor into the salt. Add ground pepper and mix well. Store in a tightly sealed glass jar or spice tin.

Recipe to Try:

SCRAMBLED EGGS IN A MUG
Try this for a quick, easy protein meal in the morning.

INGREDIENTS:

2 eggs
½ teaspoon (or to taste) Lavender French Grey sel et poivre

PREPARATION:

Lightly spray the inside of a heavy coffee mug with coconut oil cooking spray or wipe the insides with a small amount of oil. Crack eggs into the mug, add the lavender salt and pepper blend. Whip with a fork until well mixed and slightly frothy. Place the mug in a microwave oven on high for about 1 minute (ovens vary in temperature, so check the mix carefully and adjust the time as needed). The eggs will expand to the top of the mug into a light fluffy egg mix you can eat right out of the mug.

PEPPERCORN ROSE SALT

This is a textural, chunky mix that is beautiful in the bottle. To use: Sprinkle over a leafy, green salad or freshly sliced cucumbers for a zingy snack. Use this salt to season plain cream cheese or sour cream for a unique flavored vegetable dip.

INGREDIENTS:

3 tablespoons coarse grind Himalayan pink sea salt
1 tablespoon whole pink peppercorns
1 tablespoon dried red rose petals

PREPARATION:

Place all ingredients in a mortar. Use a pestle to gently grind them together until the peppercorns start to break down. Don't crush the mix into a fine powder. You can also place this in a grinder and pulse it a few times to break down the peppercorns quicker. Store in a tightly sealed glass jar.

HERB GARDEN GARLIC MIX

This is a great all-around mix that captures the flavor of an herb garden. Use this mix to season baked bread or savory cheese scones. Infuse oils and vinegars, butter or any other base that you want to add flavor to.

INGREDIENTS:

1 cup of coarse grind sea salt
1 teaspoon dried thyme
1 teaspoon dried oregano
1 teaspoon dried basil
1 teaspoon dried dill leaves
1 teaspoon dried parsley
1½ teaspoons dried garlic granules

PREPARATION:

Place all ingredients in a bowl and mix well. Crush with a pestle to break down the herbs into small pieces with the salt. You don't want the mix to be powdery, but with enough texture that is small enough to sprinkle easily through a shaker lid with large holes.

Recipe to try:

EASY HERB BEER BREAD MIX

INGREDIENTS:

3 cups flour
3¾ teaspoons baking powder
½ teaspoon salt
3 tablespoons raw sugar
½ cup grated Parmesan cheese
2 teaspoons Herb Garden Garlic Mix (recipe left)

PREPARATION:

In a large mixing bowl, whisk the ingredients together. Store the dry mix in an airtight container. (Pack this dry mix up with a recipe card and a bottle of craft beer to give as gifts.)

BREAD BAKING INSTRUCTIONS:

Preheat oven to 375° F.
Combine beer bread mix with a 12-ounce can of beer. Mix with a wooden spoon; the batter will be lumpy. Place batter in a greased loaf pan. Pour ¼ cup melted butter over the top of the loaf. Bake for 40 minutes. It is finished when it is golden brown. Remove from the oven and allow to cool for 30 minutes. Serve warm.

SALSA MIX

Use to season chopped tomatoes, onion and bell peppers for a chunky pico de gallo mix or stir the mix into crushed avocados. Can also be used to season meat for tacos.

INGREDIENTS:

2 tablespoons pepper flakes
2 tablespoons dried chives
2 tablespoons sea salt

1 teaspoon garlic granules
½ teaspoon cumin
½ teaspoon crystalized lime powder

PREPARATION:

Mix all ingredients together. Crush with a pestle to help the flavors mingle together. Store in a tightly sealed glass jar.

Recipe to try:
PICO DE GALLO

INGREDIENTS:

1 cup chopped fresh tomatoes
⅓ cup chopped fresh white onions
1 green onion, chopped
2 tablespoons cut cilantro leaves
1 to 2 teaspoons Salsa Mix
1 small can sliced black olives, drained
   (optional)

PREPARATION:

In a bowl, stir all ingredients together. Refrigerate a few hours before serving, to allow the herb mix to season the tomatoes and onions.

SAUSAGE SEASONING

Use to season fresh ground pork for a tasty breakfast sausage mix. Also good as a dry meat rub for pork roast.

INGREDIENTS:

1 teaspoon dried parsley
1½ teaspoons red Hawaiian sea salt
½ teaspoon rubbed sage (see below)

½ teaspoon dried thyme
¼ teaspoon dried ground black pepper
¼ teaspoon red pepper flakes

PREPARATION:

Mix all ingredients together well and store in a tightly sealed glass jar.

 WHAT IS RUBBED SAGE?

The term rubbed sage, used in recipes, refers to the process of taking dried whole common garden sage leaves (like the variety Berggarten or purple sage) and rubbing them until they become a light fluffy powder. The powder is used in recipes to impart a milder form of sage instead of using whole or chopped leaves.

To make rubbed sage, place a metal colander in a bowl (the bowl needs to be large enough to catch the sage falling though the holes). Place dried sage leaves in the colander. Rub the leaves with your fingertips until they disappear through the holes. Store rubbed sage in a tightly sealed glass jar.

HERBY RANCH DRESSING MIX

Easy dressing mix to make ahead. Double this recipe and store in tightly sealed jar for a ready-to-make mix all through the year.

INGREDIENTS:

1½ tablespoons dried parsley
1 tablespoon dried chives
1 teaspoon dried oregano
1 teaspoon dried thyme

1 teaspoon dried dill leaves
1 teaspoon garlic powder
1 tablespoon sea salt
¼ teaspoon ground black pepper

PREPARATION:

Combine all ingredients and store in a tightly sealed glass jar.

TO MAKE THE DRESSING:

Whisk together until smooth:
1 tablespoon Herby Ranch Dressing Mix, ½ cup mayonnaise (see homemade mayonnaise recipe on page 157) and ½ cup buttermilk – or substitute plain Green yogurt for buttermilk. If you prefer your dressing thicker, add more mayonnaise or yogurt. Refrigerate for at least an hour before serving.

YOUR SIGNATURE BLEND

Some of us simply don't have space to grow EVERY herb, so here are some easy bundles that you can turn into your own seasoning. This is a great way to join your favorite herb flavors together (and leave out flavors or textures you don't like) to personalize flavor mixes.

HOW TO:

Fresh-cut equal stem counts of two or three herbs. Tie the stems together with twine and hang the mini bundles to dry. When the bundles are completely dry, strip the herbs off the stems and into a metal tin. Add other flavors (about ¼ of the measure of herbs you have dried) like dried lemon or garlic to finish your personal mix. Crush slightly to make the herb leaves smaller and mix together well. Label with the ingredients (so you remember your own recipe!).

A gift from the garden idea: Place in a decorative tin with a culinary recipe and give your signature blends as gifts.

MIX OPTIONS FOR...

DESSERT: Lavender and lemon verbena. Add turbinado sugar in equal amount to the herbs. Nice in hot beverages and sprinkled on top of warm sugar cookies or scones.

PORK SEASONING: Sage and thyme bundled together. Add fennel seeds. Use to season ground pork or as a poultry seasoning.

CHICKEN: Tarragon and thyme bundled together. Add grated lemon peel. Mix with bread crumbs for coating on fried chicken.

BEEF: Rosemary and oregano bundled together. Add cracked pepper. Makes a nice seasoning for oven roasted meats.

SEAFOOD: Fennel and tarragon bundled together. Add dried orange peel. Use as a dry rub on salmon or ahi tuna steaks.

Recipe to try:

EASY HERBAL CHEESE CRISPS
Quick and crunchy, these make a great snack.

INGREDIENTS:

½ cup fresh grated Parmesan cheese
½ cup fresh shredded cheddar cheese
*(Or you can just use 1 cup of one
  of the above cheeses)*

1 teaspoon of your dried signature mix
  (use one of the mixes with pungent herbs like
  sage, thyme, rosemary and oregano)

PREPARATION:

Preheat oven to 350° F.
Line a flat baking sheet with
cooking parchment. In a
mixing bowl combine the
cheeses. Add the dried herb
mix to the cheese and gently
toss together. Spoon the mix
onto the baking sheet in
about a 2-inch circle shape
(about one tablespoon of
mix). Leave room between
the scoops of cheese (about
2 inches) because the circles
will melt and spread. Bake
about 7 to 10 minutes until
they are golden brown and
flattened out. Remove from
the oven and allow to cool
until crispy.

SEVEN

Rubs

Where flavor meets texture

Rubs are deep-flavored mixed herbs and spices that are used for roasting, grilling and barbeque. They are coarser than a typical seasoning salt, because you need texture and flavor that holds up to the heat of cooking. Using rubs to flavor meat is a good choice when you don't want to add the extra moisture that is typical when you use a marinade. Rubs add a crusty texture that adheres to the outside of meat to seal in flavor during cooking.

TO USE:

Dry herb rubs work best on meat that has been washed and patted dry. Massage the rub into the meat on all sides, and under skin on poultry. Allow to sit for about 30 minutes to let the flavors begin to work into the meat. Cook on a very hot grill to sear or in a hot oven during roasting to create a crispy, flavorful crust.

HERBED LIME RUB

A zesty dry rub salt wonderful on chicken and salmon. Grind this mix fine to use as a sprinkle on salads or use to season guacamole.

INGREDIENTS:

1/3 cup coarse grind French grey sea salt
1 teaspoon lime zest (add more to taste)
1 teaspoon dried garlic granules
1/4 teaspoon crystalized lime
1/2 teaspoon dried parsley, chopped
1/2 teaspoon dried chives, chopped

PREPARATION:

Mix all ingredients well. Keep the blend coarse for meat rubs. You can grind this blend down (in a spice grinder or mortar and pestle) to a finer mix for use as a seasoning salt.

BROWN SUGAR-N-SPICE RUB

Add a sweet flavor to grilling ribs or pulled pork. Make a nice glaze for ham when mixed with a little water to make thick syrup.

INGREDIENTS:

1 teaspoon red chili powder (add 1/2 teaspoon more if you like spicy heat)
1/2 teaspoon powdered cumin
1 teaspoon dried crushed oregano
1 teaspoon dried crushed lemon thyme
3 tablespoon brown sugar, packed
1/4 teaspoon black pepper
1 teaspoon ground sea salt

PREPARATION:

Mix all ingredients together. Store in a tightly sealed glass jar.

CITRUS HERB PEPPER

Tasty on pork or chicken. Sprinkle on fresh vegetables, warm pasta or salads.

INGREDIENTS:

1 tablespoon dried lemon thyme

1 tablespoon dried lemon verbena

1 tablespoon dried lemon peel

¼ teaspoon crystalized lemon

¼ teaspoon whole black peppercorns

PREPARATION:

Mix all ingredients well. Slightly crush the mix to break down the peppercorns and herbs into smaller pieces. Store in a glass jar or spice tin.

ROSEMARY SMOKED SALT

The smoky flavor of this salt tames the pungency of the rosemary for an aromatic seasoning to use with beef, pork and heavy tomato based sauces. The rosemary must be completely dry before adding to the salt. Smoked salt is found at most gourmet foods stores or online (see Resource section). My favorite in this recipe is an applewood smoked salt.

INGREDIENTS:

1 cup coarse smoked salt
¼ cup whole dried rosemary leaves
1 tablespoon dried garlic granules

PREPARATION:

In a small bowl, mix ingredients together. Transfer to a spice grinder or use a mortar and pestle to slightly crush the mix together. You want the mix to stay coarse; grinding or crushing it together will help the aromatic rosemary release into the salt and garlic. Store in a tightly sealed glass jar or spice tin.

TO USE:

GRILLED STEAKS: Generously sprinkle both sides of the steak with the mix. Press the salt mix into the meat.

ROASTS: Season pork of beef just before adding to the oven. Coat entire surface of the roast and press salt mix into the meat,

SOUPS AND SALADS: A pinch or two is yummy in tomato soup...and sprinkled on an arugula and spinach salad mix.

EIGHT

Sweet Flavor Enhancers

Breaking out of the "sugar-or-no-sugar" box and into a world of taste delights

There are many ways to sweeten foods. You can take how you sweeten your culinary treats to another level by infusing herb flavors into sugar and honey. The sweetness tames the pungent, earthy perfume taste of herbs like lavender and roses. Use flavored sugars to add an herb flavor into dessert toppings, baked goods and to sweeten beverages. Avoiding refined sugars? Infuse herbs into sweet alternatives like stevia, agave or monk fruit. Herbed honeys are easy to make and flavorful too. Once you have tried honey infusions you will find them almost magical because they are also healing infusions. The medicinal qualities of the herbs will become part of the nutritious healing qualities of the honey. Try them in hot teas to soothe coughs and sore throats or as nurturing skin care (see recipe on page 127 for a rose sea salt scrub.)

BASIC HERB SUGAR MIX

Use for sweet flavor in tea, coffee or baking.

INGREDIENTS:

Choose a single herb to infuse into sugar.
   (Use dried whole herb leaves like mint, lemon verbena,
   bee balm, scented geranium or sweet woodruff.
   Use dried flowers of lavender, chamomile, or rose petals.)
Raw turbinado, coarse or white granulated sugar

PREPARATION:

Place approximately an inch of sugar
in the bottom of a jar. Add one or two
petals or leaves, or sprinkle a layer of
herb flowers like lavender or chamomile
to cover the first layer of sugar. Repeat
sugar and herb layers until the jar is full.
Cover the top of the jar with plastic wrap
or wax paper. Let sit undisturbed for up
to two weeks.

When the sugar is heavily aromatic with
the herb, it is ready. Shake the bottle to
mix the layers together and help break
up the leaves. For a less bulky sugar, sift
the mix through a fine mesh strainer
and remove the larger pieces of herbs.
If you'd like a fine textured sugar for
baking or to sweeten frostings or cream,
pulse the mix in a grinder until it is a
fine powder. Store the aromatic sugar in
a tightly sealed glass jar.

TYPES OF SUGAR

BROWN: Light or dark brown sugar is just white sugar with molasses. The more molasses the darker the color and heavier the flavor. Brown sugars contain more moisture than a granulated white sugar, making them beneficial when baking to help cookies and breads stay chewy.

COCONUT SUGAR: A natural sugar made from coconut palm sap, it is coarse and grainy with a deep brown color. This is a good sugar for mixing with heavy-flavored spices like cinnamon.

POWDERED OR CONFECTIONER: Simply put, this is granulated sugar ground down to a fine powder. Use in recipes like whipped cream and frosting when you don't want the lingering grittiness of regular sugar.

REGULAR OR WHITE GRANULATED: The most common sugar. If a recipe does not specify a type of sugar, this is the one most often used. The small crystals are drier, which makes them less susceptible to clumping.

TURBINADO OR RAW: This is a partially processed sugar made from the juice of the sugar cane plant. It is spun and washed without removing all the molasses so it retains a light brown color. It is typically labeled as raw sugar and has a coarser texture than other sugars.

MINT SUGAR

Use to sweeten tea or rim a cocktail glass. Good for baking. Grind to a fine powder to candy edible flowers (see recipe for candied violas on page 78).

INGREDIENTS:

Mint sugar measuring ratio:
1/3 part dried chopped dried mint
2/3 part coarse-grind sugar

PREPARATION:

Blend ingredients together in a grinder, giving only a few pulses or use a mortar and pestle to grind the mint leaves into the sugar. Store in a tightly sealed glass jar.

Recipe to try:

TEQUILA MOJITO

A mojito is a traditional Cuban drink made with rum. Switch up the liquor and use silver tequila. Sweet and refreshing. For best minty-ness, the secret is in the muddling!

INGREDIENTS:

9 or 10 fresh mint leaves (whole), use spearmint if available, for a sweeter flavor
2 tablespoons fresh lime juice (typically 1 lime)
2 teaspoons fine sugar
1½ ounces silver tequila
1 cup ice cubes
½ cup club soda

PREPARATION:

Place mint leaves in a heavy glass. Add lime juice and sugar. Use a muddler to crush the mint, releasing its fragrant essential oils into the lime and sugar. Muddle just enough to crush the leaves well but not tear them into tiny shreds (it smells very minty at this point!) Pour the mint mix into a sugar-rimmed serving glass. Add ice. Pour in tequila and club soda to finish.

SWEET ROSE-LAVENDER-LEMON

A very perfumed sweetness with a zest of lemon that is good for making sweet tea. Use in baking or to dust the tops of warm sugar cookies fresh from the oven.

INGREDIENTS:

½ cup coarse raw sugar

2 tablespoons dried rose petals

1 tablespoon dried lavender buds

1 tablespoon crystallized lemon powder

PREPARATION:

Grind all ingredients in a coffee bean grinder. Store in a tightly sealed glass jar.

HOW TO SUGAR-GARNISH THE RIM OF A COCKTAIL GLASS

Place a pile of sugar on a flat plate. Cut a lime, orange or lemon into a wedge and slash it so that it will hang on the rim of a glass. Using your citrus wedge, wipe around the rim of the cocktail glass. Go around the rim a few times until it is wet with juice (the juice will help the sugar stick to the glass). Turn the glass upside down and dip the rim in the sugar until it is evenly coated.

SCENTED GERANIUM SUGAR

Sugar infused with the aroma of the geranium leaves is an earthy, sweet fragrance with the faint smell of rose. Use in baking recipes or to sweeten beverages.

PREPARATION:

Pick fresh rose-scented geranium leaves and pat dry. Place on a paper towel and allow any remnants of moisture to dry. Place approximately an inch of sugar in the bottom of a jar. Add a leaf or two on top of the sugar. Repeat leaf and sugar layers until the jar is full. Let stand up to two weeks to allow the scented geranium aroma to permeate the sugar.

Recipe to try:
GERANIUM LEMON TEA CAKE

INGREDIENTS:

2 cups flour

1½ teaspoons baking powder

¼ teaspoon salt

⅓ cup extra light olive oil

¾ cup rose geranium sugar

2 large eggs

¾ cup Greek yogurt

2 teaspoons fresh lemon verbena leaves (chopped)

2 teaspoons grated lemon zest

PREPARATION:

Preheat oven to 325°.F. Lightly oil a 9 x 5 loaf pan.

Combine flour, baking powder and salt in a bowl and set aside. In a separate bowl mix oil and sugar. Add eggs one at a time and mix well after each egg. Add the yogurt. Mix well and then add the flour mixture to the egg mix.

Gently stir and add the lemon verbena and lemon zest. Don't over-mix. Stir just enough so that all ingredients are blended in. Pour into prepared loaf pan and bake for 50 minutes or until sides pull away from the pan and bread is golden.

Lemon glaze: prepared while the loaf is cooking. Mix ½ cup of confectioner's (powdered) sugar with 3 tablespoons fresh squeezed lemon juice. Place fresh geranium leaves over the top of the loaf. While the loaf is still warm in the pan, pour the glaze over the baked loaf, covering the whole leaves. Allow to cool thoroughly before removing from the pan.

ROSEMARY INFUSED AGAVE

This is a sweet alternative to simple sugar syrup. Use as a glaze on poultry or as a cocktail sweetener. Experiment with different herbs, just one at a time. This doesn't work well with multiple herbs in one batch.

INGREDIENTS:

1 cup pure agave nectar
2 to 3 stems of the tender new growth of rosemary

PREPARATION:

Slightly warm the agave in a glass jar or bowl in the microwave. Add the rosemary to the warmed agave and pour into a sterilized glass jar. Place in the refrigerator for a few hours or overnight before use.

Sweet Syrups and Honey

ANY-HERB SIMPLE SYRUP

Simple syrup is a way to bring an herb flavor into a sweet pourable liquid. Popular for use in cocktail mixes. The sweetness can also be added to cookie dough or poured over ice cream to top it with a sweet herbal flavor.

INGREDIENTS:

2 cups granulated white sugar
2 cups water
½ cup tightly packed fresh herbs

PREPARATION:

Bring sugar and water to a boil over medium heat in a glass saucepan. Stir until sugar is completely dissolved. Remove the sugar water mix from heat and add the herbs. Allow to cool completely. Strain out the herbs through a mesh strainer and pour the syrup into a sterilized glass bottle. Store in the refrigerator and use within 2 weeks.

LAVENDER SIMPLE SYRUP

Use to flavor a latte, sparkling water, tea or cocktails.

INGREDIENTS:

2 cups fine sugar

2 cups water

½ cup fresh lavender flowers (dried can be used if fresh is not available)

PREPARATION:

Bring sugar and water to a boil over medium heat in a glass saucepan. Stir until sugar is dissolved. Remove from heat and add lavender flowers. Allow to cool completely or overnight. Strain out the lavender and pour syrup into a sterilized glass bottle. Store in the refrigerator and use within 2 weeks.

Recipe to try:
LAVENDER LEMONADE

INGREDIENTS:

1 cup fresh squeezed lemon juice

1 cup lavender simple syrup

4 cups water

PREPARATION:

Mix all the ingredients well and allow to chill for 6 hours or overnight. Garnish with a few sprigs of lemon verbena or lemon balm. Or use frozen viola ice cubes (see page 82 for recipe) for an elegant touch.

HERB HONEY INFUSION

Honey has a natural ability to draw the essence and moisture out of herb leaves, thus releasing the flavor and aroma of the herb into the honey for a sweet treat.

TO MAKE ONE PINT:

You will need about 1 cup of local, fresh raw honey and various amounts of fresh or dried herbs, depending on how large or small their leaves, petals or flowers are.

- For leafy whole herbs like mint or rose petals: fill a clean glass pint-size canning jar ½ full.
- For smaller herbs like lavender buds or chamomile flowers, fill about ⅓ of the jar.

Next, pour honey over the herbs, to the top of the jar, leaving about an inch of head space. Cover. Place honey/herb jar in a pan of water on the stove and allow the honey to become warm (do not boil). The warmth will help release the essential oils of the herbs.

Remove the honey jar from heat, cover and allow to sit for a week or longer. When the honey smells intensely of the herb, strain out the herb with a cheesecloth or mesh filter and place in a clean glass jar. Cover tightly. Honey also acts as a natural preservative due to its high sugar content and will have a long shelf life.

BEE BALM: Gives a pungent, spicy flavor to honey. Especially flavorful when infused in thick orange flower honeys. Use as a glaze on poultry.

CHAMOMILE: Sweet apple-like aroma with healing qualities, too. Use a light flavored spring honey so the honey flavor doesn't overwhelm the chamomile. Add chamomile infused honey to hot water and sip for a super sore throat healer.

LAVENDER: Adds an earthy floral taste to honey. Good for tea and in sweet cocktails blends.

LEMON VERBENA: Very mild. Adds a nice lemon aroma. Infuse into lighter spring honeys.

ROSEMARY: Use rosemary sparingly. It does not take much to permeate throughout a jar of honey. Use thicker late summer honeys and buckwheat honey. Adds a pungent flavor to honey to use as a glaze on chicken.

> **RECIPE TO TRY:** Honey mustard dipping sauce: ½ cup mayonnaise, ¼ cup mustard, ¼ cup rosemary honey. Mix together until creamy and smooth. Add a dash of salt and cayenne pepper.

MINT: Yummy drizzled on orange scones or fresh strawberries. Use in a mint julip recipe in place of simple syrup. Add to sweeten sparkling water, lemonade or tea.

ROSE: Very floral and aromatic. Nice as a glaze for baked goods and candies. A super skin healer too.

TO MAKE A SKIN-NURTURING SEA SALT SCRUB: 3 tablespoons herb infused honey, ½ cup French grey sea salt and 1 to 2 tablespoons coconut oil (just enough to make a good paste). Use as a scrub on rough skin like elbows and feet. Massage in for about 2 to 5 minutes. Rinse with water – just enough to remove graininess but not wash away the oil and honey. Pat dry and rub until the oil/honey mix disappears into skin.

TO SWEETEN HOT TEAS OR TODDIES. Honey infused with chamomile flower is perfect for this.

FOR FRUIT DIP: 2 tablespoons of herb infused honey to 1 cup plain yogurt.

FOR HONEY BUTTER: Add ¼ cup honey to ½ cup softened real butter for a spread on warm scones or use to glaze ham, chicken or vegetables.

Recipe to Try:

GLAZED CARROTS WITH LAVENDER HONEY

INGREDIENTS:

1 tablespoon butter or ghee
4 cups carrots, sliced
¼ cup lavender-infused honey
⅓ cup chicken broth
1 teaspoon orange zest

PREPARATION:

In a large skillet over medium heat, melt the butter and add carrots. Sauté a few minutes until well coated and warmed. Add remaining ingredients. Reduce heat and simmer on low until carrots are soft and the liquid has thickened. Add salt and pepper to taste.

NINE

Dressings & Condiments

Spreadable, pourable, dip-able flavor!

The recipes in this chapter are not your ordinary ketchup and mustard type of condiments, but handcrafted flavor from your herb garden. Explore the use of pesto with different herbs to not only top a bowl of warm pasta, but as a spread on breads, crackers, tortillas or pizza crust. Once you've made your own herb mayonnaise or mustard, you might never want to use store-bought again. Discover just how versatile vinegar is for making your own salad dressings or simply straight from the jar sprinkled on fresh picked spring greens. Butters, soft cream cheese and flavored oils all give diversity and creative possibilities to add herb flavoring to your culinary creations.

Most of these recipes are low to no sugar, salt or fillers that so many store-bought condiments have – perfect for healthy seasoning and restricted diet needs. You choose healthy oils and organic ingredients to let these recipes take you back to the pureness of flavor from the garden in a spreadable, pourable form.

Pesto

BASIC HERB PESTO TECHNIQUE

Pesto is commonly linked in our thoughts with the herb basil. But basil is just one of many herbs that can be made into a pesto. The origin of the word comes ffrom the Italian word *pestara*, which means to pound with a pestle. A pesto describes the action of grinding herbs and other ingredients to form a thick paste. The result is a highly concentrated way to make herbs into a sauce. The main herb used can create a pesto that is pungent or sweet.

When using small-leaf herbs like fresh thyme or rosemary, add other greens like Italian flat parsley or spinach for substance; this will create a good green base and – if you're using stronger herbs – tame their pungency.

Always use good quality extra-virgin olive oil in pesto recipes. Use a fresh batch of pesto right away, or it can be kept in the refrigerator for about 2 weeks.

You can also freeze pesto by this method: Prepare the recipe, but leave out the cheese and nuts. Spoon into small, freezer-safe canning jars, leaving about ½ inch of head space below the top of the jar. Smooth the pesto out flat with the back of a spoon. Drizzle extra-virgin olive oil over the surface until the pesto is completely sealed by the oil. Screw on a lid tightly and place in freezer. The pesto will keep for 6 months. To use: thaw and add the cheese and nuts.

ANY-HERB PESTO

This is a classic pesto recipe that you can make with whatever savory herb (or a mix of a few) that you have in the garden. Adjust the herb amount based on the pungency of the herb. For example, delicate herbs like lemon verbena and marjoram may need a greater quantity than stated in the recipe, while stronger herbs like rosemary or sage need to be adjusted to a lesser quantity.

INGREDIENTS:

About 3 cups fresh herb leaves (depending on the herb)
2 cloves fresh garlic
½ cup extra-virgin olive oil
1 teaspoon fresh lemon juice
½ to 1 teaspoon ground sea salt
2 tablespoons nuts (pine nuts, walnuts, pecans or sunflower seeds)
½ cup fresh grated Parmesan cheese

PREPARATION:

Process the herb leaves and garlic together in a food processor. Drizzle in the olive oil and blend well until smooth and creamy. Taste and adjust the flavor: Too strong? Add more oil. Not enough flavor? Add more herbs. When taste is adjusted, gently stir in the salt, nuts and cheese.

HOW TO USE PESTO:

- Toss with hot pasta, Use about ¾ cup of pesto to 1 pound of pasta.
- Add flavor to warm creamy soups. Stir about a teaspoon of pesto per cup.
- Use to stir-fry vegetables.
- For a flavorful basting sauce, mix a ratio of 1 to 1 with the leftover pan juices of baked chicken or meats.
- Use as a spread or dip on crusty bread, crackers or pita chips.

ITALIAN BASIL PESTO

The classic pesto for warm pasta. Good as a spread on pizza crust to replace the tomato sauce.

INGREDIENTS:

1½ cups large-leaf Italian basil
3 garlic cloves (or more if you like garlic)
½ cup extra-virgin olive oil
½ cup pine nuts, toasted
½ teaspoon sea salt
½ to 1 cup fresh grated Parmesan cheese

PREPARATION:

In a food processor, add basil and garlic and process, just enough to break up the garlic cloves. Drizzle in the olive oil and process until it is a smooth green paste. Remove the mix from the processor and into a mixing bowl. To toast the pine nuts: Put the nuts in a dry skillet and cook over medium heat, swirling or stirring them frequently to prevent burning. Cook for about 3 minutes. Allow to cool. Stir the nuts, salt and Parmesan cheese into the herb/olive oil mix. Use immediately or freeze.

Recipe to Try:
HEALTHY PESTO BOWL

INGREDIENTS:

1 cup cooked chicken breast, chopped into bite-size pieces
3 tablespoons Italian basil pesto (or more to taste)
1 cup cauliflower rice (cooked)
¼ cup grated Parmesan cheese

PREPARATION:

Toss the chicken and pesto together in a separate bowl. In a serving bowl, layer the ingredients: Start with the cauliflower rice on the bottom. Spread the chicken/pesto mix on top of the rice. Top with Parmesan cheese. Enjoy!

GREMOLATA

Another touch of Italy. Like pesto, gremolata is a classic Italian recipe. It is a coarse blend of parsley, garlic and lemon. Traditionally used as a garnish for Osso bucco (veal shanks). You can also use gremolata as a condiment on the side of a plate to dip fresh veggies in or as a final garnish to meat or seafood just before serving.

INGREDIENTS:

½ cup fresh Italian flat-leaf parsley, chopped
2 cloves garlic, freshly chopped
1 teaspoon lemon zest

PREPARATION:

Add all ingredients to a food processor or chop up into small pieces. The texture should be minced herbs that are not too mushy or over-processed.

If you want to experiment with more flavor, add about a tablespoon of another mild herb like tarragon, lemon verbena or marjoram. You can also tang it up with a teaspoon of capers.

TARRAGON PECAN PESTO

Nutty sweetness from the pecans combines with the delicate licorice flavor of tarragon. Use to sauté mushrooms or top scrambled eggs when they are warm in the pan.

INGREDIENTS:

¼ cup fresh tarragon leaves

½ cup fresh parsley

1 cup fresh spinach

2 garlic cloves

¼ cup extra-virgin olive oil

2 tablespoons fresh, grated Parmesan cheese

2 tablespoons toasted and chopped pecans

PREPARATION:

In a food processor, pulse the tarragon, parsley, spinach and garlic until minced. Drizzle in the olive oil and process until smooth. Add more oil if needed to make the mix thick and creamy. Stir in cheese and nuts.

SESAME HERB PESTO

A unique flavor that can be used as a spread on bread or rice crackers. Stir into fried rice or toss with fresh steamed broccoli.

INGREDIENTS:

1 pound fresh baby spinach leaves

1 cup fresh parsley leaves

¼ cup fresh chopped chives

2 to 3 fresh garlic cloves

¾ to 1 cup sesame oil

1 teaspoon sea salt

¾ cup freshly grated Parmesan cheese

Sesame seeds, toasted, as garnish

PREPARATION:

In a food processor, combine the spinach, parsley, chives and garlic cloves. Process until well mixed. Drizzle in the sesame oil until creamy. Stir in salt and cheese. Garnish with toasted sesame seeds.

LEMON/LIME PESTO

Serve this pesto on warm pasta, add shrimp and sprinkle with capers and fresh grated Parmesan cheese for an entrée.

INGREDIENTS:

1 cup fresh lemon basil leaves
¼ cup fresh lemon thyme
¼ cup fresh lemon verbena
2 cloves (or more for garlic lovers)

½ cup light olive oil
2 tablespoons fresh lime juice (about 1 lime)
1 teaspoon ground sea salt

PREPARATION:

Process lemon basil, lemon thyme, lemon verbena and garlic together in a food processor, drizzle in olive oil and blend until thoroughly pureed. Transfer to bowl and add remaining ingredients, mix well. Serve over warm pasta and garnish with the flower petals of 'Lemon Gem' marigold.

MINTY SWEET PESTO

Use this unique pesto to spread on scones, sugar cookies and muffins or as a dip for fresh fruit. Pairs nicely with roasted lamb.

INGREDIENTS:

3 cups fresh mint leaves, packed tight
¼ cup avocado or grapeseed oil

3 tablespoons honey
Chopped pecans or almonds, if desired

PREPARATION:

Chop mint leaves in a food processor. Drizzle in oil and process until creamy and smooth. Add more oil if needed to make a smooth paste. Stir in honey and nuts.

Vinegars

Making herbal vinegars is a simple way to create low-fat and low-calorie flavorings for salads, marinades and culinary dishes. Most flavored herbal vinegars can be substituted in recipes that call for plain vinegar or lemon juice.

They are also an easy and flavorful way to craft elegant gifts from your garden. Pour finished herb vinegars into a decorative bottle and label with a recipe for use. Discover how versatile herbal vinegars can be too. Herb infused vinegars are used for skin cleansing tonics and even aromatic household cleansers. See the recipe for an Eco-friendly cleaner on page 55 using rosemary and other cleansing herbs.

BASIC HERB VINEGAR

Sprinkle over cooked or raw vegetables for fresh seasoning. Add vinegar as a marinade to meat or poultry as it is roasting. The vinegar will tenderize and season the meat as it cooks. Use straight out of the bottle as salad dressing on leafy greens, pasta, potatoes and other vegetables. Blend the herb vinegar with olive oil for a creamy dressing to use on warm pastas or deli sandwiches.

INGREDIENTS:

1 cup fresh, firmly packed herbs
2 cups vinegar
Large, clean, sterilized glass jar for brewing
Decorative bottles for finished storage (clean and sterilized)

PREPARATION:

Gently wash herbs. Remove any discolored or damaged leaves and stems. Allow to air dry thoroughly. It is important not to introduce moisture from herbs, flowers and other edibles or the vinegar may cloud up. Pack the washed, dry herbs into a clean, sterilized glass jar.

Pour the vinegar into the jar. With a wooden spoon (do not use metal utensils) push on the herbs to help gently crush and bruise them and release their essential oils into the vinegar. Cover the jar mouth with parchment or plastic wrap, then screw on the lid. Do not allow the vinegar to come in contact with a metal lid. Shake the mix well and allow to steep for up to 4 weeks in a cool, dark place. Do a taste or sniff test every week to determine if it is ready; after a few weeks add more herbs if a stronger flavor is desired.

When the mix is ready, strain out the herbs through a mesh screen or cheesecloth. Throw away or compost the old vinegar-soaked herbs. Pour the herbal vinegar into decorative bottles. For a special touch, add fresh stems of herbs to the vinegar before sealing the jar. Properly stored herb vinegars may be kept up to 12 months. The recipe is easily doubled for gift-making batches.

Note: If you want to make a vinegar but only have dried herbs to use, you can use a ratio of 1 cup of dried herbs to about 3 cups of vinegar.

WHICH VINEGAR?

Vinegars are sharp or sour-tasting acidic liquids made from the fermentation of fruits or berries – or grains like rice. Each of these base ingredients gives its own unique flavor and fragrance to create different types of herb vinegars. The varying levels of acid and fragrance also make some more valuable for household and cosmetic use.

BALSAMIC VINEGAR: A deep, rich, dark-colored vinegar with an intense fruity flavor. Best used with heavy, pungent herbs and spices. Use in meat marinades and heavy sauces to take advantage of its rich flavor.

CHAMPAGNE VINEGAR: A clear, light vinegar ideal for culinary herbal blends. It is nice for delicate flower vinegars like chive blossoms and nasturtiums.

CIDER VINEGAR: This caramel-colored vinegar is commonly used in salad dressings and in combination with stronger flavored herbs. It also has many medicinal and health benefits and is used to infuse herbs for medicinal and cosmetic use.

RED WINE VINEGAR: Pale red color and tart flavor – better for robust herbs that have heavy flavor like rosemary, oregano and garlic, and spices like peppercorns or chilies.

RICE VINEGAR: A sweet, clear vinegar that readily picks up flavors of delicate herbs. Nice for fruit vinegars like raspberry and blueberry. Use rice vinegar if you have an aversion to a strong vinegar smell.

WHITE DISTILLED VINEGAR: This is a common vinegar distilled from petroleum, grain or a wood by-product. This is best used as a base for herbal household cleaning and not preferred for edible herb vinegar infusions. (See page 55 for an herbal household cleaner.)

WHITE WINE VINEGAR: A lighter, more delicate flavor that is excellent for delicate herbs and fruits.

BASIL VINEGAR

Use as a dressing on leafy salads, or add a splash to a Bloody Mary cocktail recipe to add a flavorful herb zing. 'Dark Opal' or 'Red Rubin' basil will infuse a delicate pink color into the vinegar.

INGREDIENTS:

2 cups leafy Italian basil
2 cups white wine or champagne vinegar
About 10 whole black peppercorns.

PREPARATION:

Gently wash the basil leaves. Allow to air dry thoroughly. Add the basil leaves and peppercorns into a clean, sterilized glass jar. Pour the vinegar over the leaves. With a wooden spoon push gently to crush and bruise the basil leaves to release their essential oils. Stir the mix well.

Cover the jar mouth with parchment or plastic wrap then screw on the lid. Let steep for up to 4 weeks in a cool dark place. Do a taste or sniff test after a few weeks and add more basil if a stronger flavor is desired. When the vinegar has a highly aromatic basil smell, it is ready. Strain out the leaves and peppercorns through cheesecloth. Pour the herbal vinegar into decorative bottles.

Recipe to try:

BASIL VINAIGRETTE

Perfect to dress up a bowl of fresh vegetables, pasta or salad.

INGREDIENTS:

½ cup extra-virgin olive oil
2 tablespoon basil vinegar
¼ cup chopped green onions

1 garlic clove
Salt and pepper

PREPARATION:

In a blender or food processor, mix the olive oil and basil vinegar. Add remaining ingredients and continue blending until smooth and creamy. Add more olive oil if needed to create a nice pouring consistency. Add salt and pepper to taste. Store in the refrigerator. Best used within a week.

DILLY ZEST VINEGAR

Yummy on coleslaw. Mix with mayonnaise to season yolks for deviled eggs.

INGREDIENTS:

3 leafy stems fresh dill
2 teaspoons dill seed
3 cloves garlic
2 cups cider vinegar

PREPARATION:

Add dill, dill seed and garlic to a sterilized glass quart canning jar. Add vinegar and make sure all ingredients are submerged in the liquid. Use the back of a wooden spoon to crush the cloves. Stir the mix well. Seal tight and allow to steep for about 4 weeks. Strain and bottle in a decorative bottle. Add a fresh stem of leafy dill and a lemon ribbon (a long narrow peel of lemon) to the bottle for garnish.

NASTURTIUM FLOWER VINEGAR

Nice and peppery, use this as a dressing or a splash over fresh vegetables.

INGREDIENTS:

2 cups nasturtium petals
About 5 to 10 whole black peppercorns
3½ cups white wine vinegar

PREPARATION:

Add all the ingredients to a sterilized glass quart canning jar, and stir with a bamboo skewer or chopstick. Seal with a lid and allow to steep for about 6 weeks. Strain off the petals through a mesh filter or cheesecloth and rebottle in a decorative bottle.

Recipe to try:

EASY OIL AND VINEGAR DRESSING

INGREDIENTS:

1 cup olive or avocado oil to ⅓ cup nasturtium vinegar

PREPARATION:

Pour together in a jar. Store in the refrigerator. Shake well before each use.

CHIVE BLOSSOM VINEGAR

The color of the blossom will add an attractive pale pink color to the vinegar. This is a pungent vinegar that has a strong chive aroma. Add to salad dressing mixes calling for vinegar. Sprinkle on warm pasta or freshly sliced cucumbers.

INGREDIENTS:

6 whole chive blossoms
2 cups white wine vinegar
About 6 to 10 whole peppercorns
    for garnish

PREPARATION:

Gently wash the flowers, put into a sterilized bottle and poor in vinegars. With a wooden spoon, gently crush the flowers in the vinegar. Allow to sit for about 2 weeks or until the vinegar smells heavily of chives and picks up the color of the blossoms. Strain off the flowers and rebottle the vinegar. Garnish the bottle of vinegar with fresh chive blossoms and whole peppercorns.

Flavored Herb Oils

Base oils like avocado oil, olive oil and grapeseed oil have mild to little flavor on their own, but infuse herbs into them and they become a culinary specialty item. These are low-smoke-point oils, so they're not used for high heat cooking or frying. Use your delicate homemade flavored oils for dipping bread, flavoring condiments, stirring into simmering soups and tossing with steamed vegetables.

OIL SAFETY

Infusing fresh herbs in oil increases the risk of botulism. Garlic adds an even higher risk. Herb infused oils with fresh herbs can also mold quickly. Store herb oils in the refrigerator. Make small batches and use the flavored oil within a week. Herbs that are completely dried and then infused into the oil are less at risk for growing botulism spores. Use flavored herb oils made with dried herbs within a few months. Always use sterilized clean glass jars and utensils for preparation and bottling.

BASIC HERB OIL INFUSION

For leafy, tender herbs like basil, young parsley, cilantro and tarragon, use about 1 cup of fresh packed leaves to 2 cups of oil.

For woody, pungent herbs like sage, rosemary, thyme and oregano, use 3 to 4 cups of leaves to 2 cups of oil.

If using fresh herbs, make a small batch and use the oil right away. Use dried herbs for a longer shelf life and to decrease the risk of the oil going bad. (See safety notes above.)

In a sterilized quart-sized glass jar, add herbs and oil. Mix well and with a wooden spoon crush the herbs into the oil to help release their flavor and aroma.

METHODS TO INFUSE OILS

NO-HEAT METHOD: Place in a sunny window or warm spot for a week. Check the fragrance and flavor and allow to steep for longer if needed. When the oil is heavily aromatic and flavorful with the herb, it is ready.

STOVETOP: Use a saucepan large enough to hold the bottle you are using for the herbs and oil. Fill the pan about 1/3 with water. Heat water to a simmer. Add jar with oil and herb mix. Simmer for about an hour or two. The heat will help release the herb essence into the oil. Remove the jar from the pan and allow to cool completely.

MICROWAVE: in a glass microwave-safe wide-mouth jar, heat just the oil until it is warm, about 150°F (use a candy thermometer to check the temperature). Do not overheat the oil and use caution when removing the jar from the oven. Add the herbs to the warmed oil and push in with a bamboo skewer to make sure that all the herbs are completely submerged in the oil. Allow to cool completely.

FOR ALL METHODS: Strain the oil through a mesh strainer or cheesecloth to remove the herb leaves. Pour the oil into a clean, sterilized bottle. Store infused oils in the refrigerator and use within 1 one week to a few months (depending on your use of dried or fresh herbs, see safety notes).

MUSTARD SAUCE

INGREDIENTS:

2 teaspoons dry mustard
½ cup Dijon-style mustard
¼ cup herbed vinegar
⅓ cup herb oil

2 tablespoons chopped dried herb
(use an herb that complements or is the same one that is used in the oil and vinegar in this recipe)

PREPARATION:

Combine ingredients and stir until creamy. Store in a glass jar and refrigerate. Use within a week.

ROSEMARY OIL

Use straight on salad as a dressing or brush on meat just before adding a spice rub. Nice for its medicinal properties too. Rosemary has pain relieving qualities and the oil can be massaged on sore joints and muscles to relieve pain. **Note:** *for skin care, use sweet almond oil or grapeseed oil to avoid the stronger fragrance of olive oil.*

INGREDIENTS:

2 cups grapeseed oil or extra-virgin olive oil.
1 cup fresh rosemary sprigs (use tender stems cut from new growth)

PREPARATION:

Snip the rosemary in small pieces (tender stems can be cut up and used), and strip the leaves from woody stems. Fill a quart jar ½ to ¾ full of freshly snipped herb. Pour the oil over the herbs and fill the jar to the top. You can slightly warm the oil before pouring onto the herb to help release the essential oils. Stir the oil well and gently bruise the rosemary leaves with the base of a wooden spoon to help release the flavorful essential oils. Cover jar tightly. Allow to steep in the refrigerator for a week before use. Strain out the herbs through a cheesecloth. Re-bottle the oil in clean sterilized glass, seal tightly and label. Store in the refrigerator.

MEDITERRANEAN GARDEN OIL

A mix of pungent herbs native to the Mediterranean region. Rich and flavorful. Use this as a bread dipping oil or drizzle on your favorite mix of olives.

INGREDIENTS:

2 cups extra-virgin olive oil
¼ cup dried whole leaf oregano
½ cup dried basil leaves
¼ cup dried savory leaves
½ cup dried parsley
¼ cup dried rosemary
Whole black peppercorns

PREPARATION:

Place all the dried herbs and peppercorns in a quart-size glass jar. In a separate glass measuring cup, warm the oil in a microwave oven. Do not overheat. Each oven's timing is different so check the oil every 30 seconds until very warm, but not burning hot.

Pour the warm oil into the quart jar to completely submerge the herbs. With a wooden spoon, crush the herbs into the oil. Stir to mix well. Place the herb-and-oil-filled jar in a pan of simmering water for about 3 minutes. Remove from heat and allow to cool completely. Strain the oil through a fine mesh strainer or cheesecloth to remove the remnants of the herb leaves. Pour oil into a narrow bottle and seal tightly. Store in the refrigerator.

ORANGE-FLAVORED OLIVE OIL

INGREDIENTS:

1 cup extra-virgin olive oil
2 oranges (peels only)

PREPARATION:

Place oil and orange peels in a blender. Whirl until well mixed and the peels are finely chopped. Allow to sit for about an hour. Strain through a mesh cheesecloth to remove bits of the orange peel. Store in a tightly sealed glass jar in the refrigerator.

Recipe to Try:
ORANGE MARJORAM VINAIGRETTE

Nice tossed on spinach salad with bacon bits and hard-boiled eggs.

INGREDIENTS:

¼ cup orange-flavored olive oil (purchased or see recipe)
2 tablespoons balsamic vinegar
1 teaspoon dried marjoram
¼ teaspoon salt
¼ teaspoon pepper

PREPARATION:

Place all ingredients in a glass jar, seal with a lid and shake well. Can also be whirled in a blender until well mixed and frothy. Use immediately or store in a tightly sealed glass jar and use within a week.

HERB-N-OIL PASTE

Herbal pastes are thick, spreadable blends of fresh herbs and oil. The oil is basically a carrier to make an herb into a flavorful and aromatic paste. Best made with one individual herb. Use pastes for sautéing, baking, soups and stir-fry.

PREPARATION:

Wash and pat dry whole herb leaves. Start with one cup tightly packed leaves.

Place herbs in a food processor and chop. Slowly drizzle in oil until the mixture becomes a thick paste. For heavy flavors such as basil, cilantro or parsley, use flavorful olive oil. For delicate flavors such as mint, thyme or lemon verbena use coconut oil.

Transfer the mix to a zip-close freezer bag, squeeze out the air and flatten. Seal well and freeze. To use: break off frozen chunks as needed. Melt into sauces, soups and other warm liquids.

For easy use in recipes: Place a measured amount, such as a tablespoon, into each section of an ice cube tray. After the cubes have frozen store them in a freezer bag. You will have a measured amount to add to cooking. Herb-n-oil pastes will last 6 months to a year in the freezer.

BASE OILS FOR HERBS

AVOCADO OIL: Popular because it is a rich oil that is high in "good fat" (monounsaturated). It has a high smoke point and can be used for roasting, searing and stir-fry.

COCONUT OIL: This oil is extracted from the meat of mature coconuts. The oil is solid at room temperature and will melt on surfaces and air temperature at about 80° F. It is not good for pouring oils. Use for mixes that are heavier and spreadable like herb pastes and pestos.

GRAPESEED OIL: A pretty, light green oil that has a high smoke point, so it can be used for sautéing and stir-fry. It has a clean, clear, taste and little aroma, so it works well when you want to have a strong herb flavor without the oil distracting from the taste. Nice for vinaigrette blends.

OLIVE OIL: For infusing and crafting herb oils, there are two types of olive oil to become familiar with. Pure or regular olive oil has a lighter more neutral taste and color with a higher smoke point, so it can be used in dishes that are heated up. Extra-virgin olive oil has a more robust flavor and aroma. The flavor can vary based on what region of the world the olives originate from. Don't use extra-virgin olive oil for high temperature cooking. Extra-virgin olive oil adds flavor to stronger herbs like sage, thyme, savory and rosemary.

SESAME OIL: This oil has the light, nutty flavor of sesame seeds. Use it for any type of herbs and especially in Asian dishes and recipes with citrus in them. Good flavor to use in salad dressings. It can be used for sautéing, but not high-heat frying.

Butters

Adding herbs to butter is an aromatic and colorful culinary treat with unlimited options for flavor combinations. The fat in butter picks up the essence of the herbs well. The butter will become stronger the more herbs that you use. Herb butters can be frozen to keep them longer: Fill sections of an ice cube tray full of herb butter mix, freeze until solid, then remove from the tray and store in freezer-safe containers. For use: Melt cubes while sautéing meats, seafood and scrambled eggs.

BASIC HERB BUTTER

Experiment with one herb or blend two together to create a flavorful spread for breads, crackers, baking and sautéing.

INGREDIENTS:

1 cube (½ cup) unsalted butter
1 teaspoon lemon juice
2 to 3 tablespoons fresh herbs

PREPARATION:

Soften butter, add remaining ingredients. Cream together well, place in tightly covered container and refrigerate at least 3 hours or overnight for best flavor. Store in the refrigerator and use within 2 weeks.

CHIVE BUTTER

The classic herb butter blend for a baked potato topper or to spread on corn on the cob.

INGREDIENTS:

1 cube (½ cup) salted butter
1 teaspoon lemon juice
2 to 3 tablespoons fresh chives, chopped

PREPARATION:

Soften butter, add remaining ingredients, cream together well, place in tightly covered container. Refrigerate at least 3 hours or overnight for best flavor. Store in the refrigerator and use within 2 weeks.

PEPPERY DILL & BEE BALM BUTTER

Pretty and peppery. Use on crackers or spread onto fish before baking.

INGREDIENTS:

1 cube (½ cup) salted butter, softened
1 tablespoon fresh dill leaves
1 teaspoon grated lemon zest

¼ teaspoon ground black pepper
2 to 3 bee balm flowers

PREPARATION:

Combine butter dill, lemon zest and black pepper in a bowl. Stir well until creamy. Set aside.

Prepare the mold for the butter: Line the inside of a small, square-shaped bowl, mini cake tin or butter mold with plastic wrap. Gently remove the petals from the bee balm flower heads and sprinkle them onto the plastic wrap in the tin. Spoon softened butter mix into mold, gently pressing down to embed the bee balm petals as the butter shapes itself to the mold. Turn the mold over onto a small plate and remove the plastic wrap.

POPPY SEED LEMON VERBENA BUTTER ROUNDS

INGREDIENTS:

1 cup unsalted butter, softened
¼ cup lemon juice
½ teaspoon lemon zest

¼ cup fresh lemon verbena leaves, minced
Poppy seeds

PREPARATION:

In a mixing bowl, combine butter, lemon juice, lemon zest and lemon verbena leaves. Mix until smooth and creamy. Place softened butter on waxed paper. Form the butter into a log roll shape about 2 inches in diameter. If butter is very soft, place in the refrigerator to make it more workable. Once you have a nice rounded log, roll it in poppy seeds to lightly coat the outside. Wrap in wax paper and place in refrigerator until firm. Remove the wax paper and slice the butter log into disks, using a warm butter knife. Wipe the knife after each cut to keep the cut edge tidy.

FLOWER GARDEN BUTTER

Sweet and flowery. Use to spread on sweet breads, pancakes and warm muffins.

INGREDIENTS:

1 cup unsalted butter, softened
3 tablespoons mint leaves, minced
1 teaspoon rose water (purchased or see recipe below)
½ teaspoon lime zest
1 tablespoon raspberry or strawberry preserves
Fresh, organic, pink or red roses or violas to use as garnish

PREPARATION:

Combine butter, mint leaves, rose water and lime zest until creamy and smooth.

Stir in fruit preserves. Using a clear glass bowl, decorate the inside with rose petals and violas. Use a small dab of butter to help the flowers stick in place. Add the remaining butter into the bowl and smooth the surface. Garnish the top with flowers. Cover and chill for 2 days.

ROSE WATER

INGREDIENTS:

2 cups distilled water
1 overflowing cup rose petals (about 2 to 3 roses)

PREPARATION:

Prepare the rose petals by cutting off the white bitter end of the petal (where they were connected to the base of the flower). Use only organic, fragrant roses. Place distilled water in a small glass saucepan. Add the prepared rose petals and push them into the water so they are all submerged. Cover the pan and simmer the rose/water mix for about 20 to 30 minutes. Remove from heat and strain through a cheesecloth or mesh strainer to remove the petals from the water. Allow to cool completely, cover tightly and store in the refrigerator.

Mustard & Mayo

Move beyond boring mustard and mayonnaise! Use earthy, piquant herbs from the garden like thyme, rosemary, savory and sage to create your own specialty mayonnaise blends. Making mustard is easy and quick and like anything handcrafted, much better than store-bought.

TARRAGON MUSTARD

Typically, an expensive specialty mustard in specialty stores, you can make your own fresh batch for pennies. Use on roasted chicken or stir into a cream sauce for sautéed mushrooms.

INGREDIENTS:

¼ cup light mustard seeds
¼ cup white wine vinegar
¼ cup dry white wine
¼ cup water

1 tablespoon honey
2 tablespoons fresh tarragon leaves, minced
½ clove garlic, minced
½ teaspoon salt

PREPARATION:

In a glass canning jar, combine the mustard seeds, vinegar, wine and water. Do not cover the jar. Allow to sit for 3 hours. In a separate bowl combine the honey, tarragon and garlic. Mix well. Let sit for an hour. Combine both mixes into a food processor and process to a creamy texture.

Using a double boiler over simmering water, place the mustard mix in the top pan. Stir in the salt and cook, stirring often, until mustard starts to thicken up – about 10 to 15 minutes. Mustard will thicken up more after it has cooled. Pour into a sterilized glass jar and allow to cool. Cover tightly and store in the refrigerator. Wait a few days before use to allow the flavors to mingle.

HERB GARDEN SPICY BROWN MUSTARD

Tangy and easy to make, add other herbs you have in the garden for more flavor.

INGREDIENTS:

1 cup white wine vinegar
¾ cup brown mustard seeds
1 tablespoon dry mustard powder
1 teaspoon sea salt
¼ teaspoon ground allspice

¼ teaspoon ground ginger
¼ teaspoon fresh dill leaves, minced
¼ teaspoon fresh thyme leaves, minced
¼ teaspoon fresh parsley leaves, minced

PREPARATION:

In a small jar, place the mustard seeds and the vinegar together and allow the seeds to soak at least 4 hours. Pour mustard seed and vinegar mix into a blender or food processor and add the remaining ingredients. Mix until the consistency you like, from slightly seedy (blended just a few minutes) to creamy smooth (blended for about 5 minutes.) If the mix is too thick, add some water until the right consistency is achieved. Pour into a small glass jar and cap tightly. Store in the refrigerator. The mustard will become more flavorful if you allow it to sit for about a week before using. Use within a month.

HOMEMADE MAYONNAISE

INGREDIENTS:

1 large egg yolk
1½ teaspoons fresh lemon juice
1 teaspoon white wine vinegar
¼ teaspoon Dijon mustard

¾ cup avocado oil
½ teaspoon (or more) dried herbs
Salt to taste (start with ¼ teaspoon)

PREPARATION:

Combine egg yolk, lemon juice and vinegar in a bowl. Whisk until well blended. Continue whisking and begin to slowly drizzle in the oil. Take your time drizzling in the oil – the slower the better, up to 10 minutes. This helps the oil mix well into the other ingredients. Once the mix is blended and fluffy, stir in the herbs and salt. Spoon into a glass jar, cover tightly and store in the refrigerator. Use within a few weeks. *Note:* consuming raw egg yolks might increase your risk of foodborne illness.

HERB-INFUSED MAYO

PREPARATION:

Make a basic homemade mayonnaise recipe (recipe above).

When the mayonnaise is finished, you can infuse herbs into it to flavor it any way you like. Just add about a ½ teaspoon or more of dried herbs, whip into the mayonnaise and allow to sit overnight before use.

Soft Cheese

Choose your flavor, savory or sweet! Use this basic recipe to make a rich cream cheese spread to use in cooking or served fresh as a spread on bagels or for a vegetable dip. If you want to experiment with another type of cheese, choose soft cheeses like brie, Neufchâtel or ricotta. In a sweet recipe substitute an edible flower or herb like lavender or lemon verbena to create your own signature blend.

BASIC HERBAL CREAM CHEESE
Serve on crackers, bagels or warm breadsticks.

INGREDIENTS:

8-ounce package cream cheese, softened

1 to 2 tablespoons chopped fresh herb

PREPARATION:

Cream together ingredients until well mixed. Refrigerate overnight. Garnish with dried chopped herb on the surface of the cheese.

SWEET FLORAL CREAM CHEESE
A yummy fruit dip for strawberries or spread on tea sandwiches or scones.

INGREDIENTS:

8-ounce package cream cheese, softened
4 tablespoons confectioner's sugar

2 overflowing tablespoons fresh rose petals, snipped into small pieces

PREPARATION:

Cream together the cream cheese and sugar until smooth. Stir in the rose petals until mixed well. Refrigerate overnight.

TEN

Beverages

From infused waters and teas to botanical cocktails

D rink your herbs! Try these plant-based adventures to mix and experiment with all the ways you can drink herbal flavor. Start with easy and flavorful herb infused waters with fresh fruits for healthy, flavorful hydration. Fizzy herb sodas are easy to mix with herb sugar syrups from Chapter 9. Season wine for sipping or cooking by infusing herbs and spices. Botanical cocktails add a new level of flavor when you impart fresh herbs into liquor like whiskey and vodka. Make a toast at your next summer party with Hedgerow Fizz. And of course, a classic beverage warm or chilled with ice, herbal teas are both healing and flavorful. Let the infusions begin!

Herb Infused Waters
tasty, healthy hydration!

Why buy flavored waters when you can make your own? As with crafting all things using fresh plants from the garden, you get to choose the ingredients and quality. Leave out the things you don't want, like extra sugar or additives. Water infusions are not intended to be heavy and sweet. The light, refreshing hint of fruits and herbs should satisfy thirst without overwhelming the taste buds. Fresh-made herbal waters are a great way to stay hydrated through the day, with some micro benefits from the fresh herbs. Cool, infused waters are a healthy alternative to sugary or caffeine-laden drinks.

All beverage recipes here are measured to use a half-gallon wide-mouth glass canning jar. This is a good size to make small batches. Plus, they aren't so heavy and awkward to pour from like gallon glass jars can be. For bigger batches, simply double the recipes and infuse in a gallon glass jar.

DIRECTIONS FOR ALL WATER INFUSIONS:

Once you add the ingredients and stir as indicated, fill the jar with water to the neck of the jar (leave a few inches of head space for the rim.) Screw the lid on tightly and place in the refrigerator. For best flavors, steep for a minimum of 6 to 12 hours before drinking.

TIPS FOR MAKING
HERB-FLAVORED WATER INFUSIONS

- To strain the water as you pour, use a screw-on mesh lid (typically used for draining sprouting jars) found in kitchen supply stores, or see the Resources section at the back of the book.

- Before adding lemons, oranges or limes to the water, remove the citrus peels and white pith to avoid bitterness.

- Woody spices will infuse better if crushed first.

- Strain out the bits and pieces of ingredients from the jar or use a mesh lid to pour from. Use the strained-out herbs and fruits from the water to make smoothies.

- Cut fruits into thick, chunky pieces so that small pieces don't turn to mush

- Experiment with flavor; you can use coconut water or green tea in place of plain water.

- Muddle tough, leafy herbs to help them release flavor into the water (see sidebar next page).

- Use cold or room temperature water (not warm or hot).

CUCUMBER LIME MINT

INGREDIENTS:

1 cucumber, peeled and sliced
8 to 10 whole fresh mint leaves
Juice of 1 small lime

1 teaspoon mint sugar syrup, if desired for
for sweetness (see recipe on page 124)

PREPARATION:

Add cucumber to the glass jar. In a separate small glass bowl, pour in about ½ cup of water. Add the mint leaves and muddle them into the water. Pour muddled mint water over the cucumbers. Add lime juice (and mint sugar syrup, if desired) and fill the jar with water. Stir all ingredients with a wooden spoon. Cover and infuse.

HOW TO MUDDLE HERBS

Get a muddler. A muddler is a long, narrow utensil that is rounded on the end and is typically made of wood. It is long enough to go into a glass but wide enough to be able to crush leaves and harder ingredients like salt or peppercorns. To start, you need a heavy glass or jar, you will be pressing against it, so the glass needs to be sturdy. Place the herb leaves in the bottom of the glass or jar. Add a small amount of sugar, water, fruit or another ingredient of the recipe you want to infuse the herb's flavor into. Place your muddler in the glass and press on the herbs with a twisting motion. It doesn't take much effort. You don't want to tear up the leaves, you are just pressing hard on them to release their essential oils. You will know it is working when your ingredients are heavily fragranced with the herb.

PINEAPPLE GINGER

INGREDIENTS:

2 to 3 cups fresh pineapple, cut into large cubes

1 teaspoon fresh grated ginger – add more if you like more taste of fresh ginger

5 to 6 whole fresh mint leaves

Juice of 1 small lime

PREPARATION:

Add all the ingredients to the glass jar. Fill with water, stir, cover and infuse.

STRAWBERRY LEMON

INGREDIENTS:

3 cups fresh strawberries, sliced in half

½ cup fresh lemon verbena leaves

4 to 5 fresh lemon balm leaves

1 lemon, sliced with the peel removed

PREPARATION:

Add all the ingredients to the glass jar. Fill with water, stir, cover and infuse.

RASPBERRY BASIL

INGREDIENTS:

2 to 3 cups raspberries

8 basil leaves

½ orange, sliced with the peel removed

PREPARATION:

Add all the ingredients to the glass jar. Fill with water, cover and infuse.

LAVENDER BLUEBERRY

INGREDIENTS:

2 to 3 cups blueberries
3 tablespoons fresh lavender flowers
1 lemon, sliced with the peel removed

PREPARATION:

Place blueberries in the glass jar. Lightly crush them with the back of a spoon or ladle to break open their skins (no need to completely smash them). Place lavender flowers in a tea mesh infuser (see Resources section) or wrap in cheesecloth bundle. Add lavender bundle and lemon to the jar. Fill with water, stir, cover and infuse.

BORAGE AND CUCUMBER WATER

INGREDIENTS:

12 to 15 borage flowers
1 lemon, sliced with the peel removed
1 cucumber, peeled and sliced
A few sprigs fresh lemon thyme

PREPARATION:

Add all the ingredients to the glass jar. Fill with water, cover and infuse.

Make your herb waters fizzy! Add all the ingredients according to the recipe, but fill the jar only half with water. This will make a concentrated flavor infusion. After steeping for at least 6 hours, fill the jar the rest of the way with club soda or seltzer water. Serve immediately.

LAVENDER HERB SODA

Refreshing and fizzy, use lavender or try another herb sugar syrup (see recipe on page 124) to customize the flavor.

INGREDIENTS:

½ cup fresh squeezed lime juice

25 ounces sparkling mineral water

1 cup Lavender Sugar Syrup
   (see recipe on page 125)

PREPARATION:

Add ingredients to a serving pitcher and stir to mix well. Serve immediately over ice and garnish with a lavender stem.

Tea

For centuries herbaceous plants have been steeped in water to capture all the aroma and qualities of the essential oils in plants to help enhance sleep, settle a distressed tummy or to calm and soothe the body and soul. Some define tea as a beverage, hot or cold, made only from the leaves of *Camellia sinensis*, but the word "tea" is also used in a general way to describe a drink made by steeping herb leaves, flowers or seeds in hot water. When it comes to herbs steeped in water, these aromatic blends made from herbs are also known as tisanes or infusions. Making your own blends is a way to capture the aroma and flavor of herbs from your garden. The herbs used in these recipes do not contain caffeine and added sugars, making these teas healthy and flavorful.

HERB TEA FLAVOR INFUSION GUIDE

FENNEL SEED: Very aromatic with a spicy, warming flavor.

LAVENDER: Its earthy, perfume aroma mixes well with other florals like roses. Very nice with chamomile.

LEMON GRASS: Mild lemony flavor has a hint of zest, almost like ginger. Add to chamomile or lemon teas.

MARJORAM LEAF: Pungent yet sweet, pair with lemon verbena or mints for a refreshing aftertaste.

MINT LEAF: Makes a rich, green-colored tea, very aromatic and flavorful all alone. Blends well with other herbs in dried tea mixes.

PARSLEY: For a nice simple, green herbal flavor rich in vitamins. Add a squeeze of lime for a unique zippy flavor.

ROSE PETALS: The aromatic, rose perfume adds sweetness to teas. Nice to blend with other florals and rose-scented geranium leaves.

SWEET WOODRUFF: The leaves of sweet woodruff, when dried, have a vanilla-like flavor. Very mild and flavorful when sweetened with honey.

BASIL: Very aromatic with a bit of clove flavor. Nice all alone or mixed with spices like cinnamon.

BEE BALM: Use the leaves as an addition to mints, lavender and citrus-y herb blends. Very aromatic when subjected to heat.

CHAMOMILE: Popular pale yellow tea with a faint apple honey-like flavor. Add raw honey to sweeten and enhance its natural flavor.

ELDERFLOWER: With its touch of vanilla aroma, elderflower is best in combination with other herbs like mint, or florals like roses.

DRIED TEA MIXES

Make tea blends to store in your tea cabinet so you can enjoy the flavors of your herb garden any time of year. Double or triple the recipe ingredients to make larger batches to package and give as gifts.

FLORAL TEA

INGREDIENTS:

2 teaspoons dried chamomile flowers
2 teaspoons dried rose petals

1 teaspoon dried lavender buds

PREPARATION:

Mix all together well. Store in a tin or glass jar in a dark cabinet. Use an overflowing teaspoon per cup of water.

HERBAL CITRUS TEA

INGREDIENTS:

3 teaspoons dried lemon verbena leaves
2 teaspoons dried bee balm leaves
1 teaspoon dried lemongrass

½ teaspoon dried orange peel,
   with white pith removed

PREPARATION:

Break the leaves into small pieces and mix with the lemongrass and orange peel. Store in a tin or glass jar in a dark cabinet. Use an overflowing teaspoon per cup of water.

MINT GERANIUM TEA

INGREDIENTS:

4 teaspoons dried peppermint leaves

1 teaspoon dried rose geranium leaves

PREPARATION:

Break down the leaves together into small pieces so the two leaf flavors mix well. Store in a tin or glass jar in a dark cabinet. Use an overflowing teaspoon per cup of water.

STEEPING HERBS

ANOTHER HERB TEA OPTION: Use a favorite type of tea such as green tea or Darjeeling. In a gallon glass jar, add 6 tea bags and 1 cup of fresh herb leaves. Steep in the sun as above recipe. Filter out the tea bags and herbs before serving. Serve with herbal ice cubes.

A note for tea blending: Dried herbs are more concentrated. If you are brewing tea with fresh leaves follow this rule of thumb: 1 teaspoon of dried or 3 teaspoons of fresh to 1 cup of water.

HOW TO BREW FRESH HERB TEA

Boil water in a teakettle. Transfer boiling water into a warmed glass or ceramic teapot. Add a handful of fresh herb leaves and allow to steep for at least 10 minutes, or longer if a stronger tea is desired. If you are using dried herbs, use about one well rounded teaspoon of broken herb leaves or flowers per cup of water.

Most herbal blends do not reach a deep dark color; they will remain light amber or green. Gauge your herbal brew by taste rather than by color.

HOW TO BREW FRESH HERBAL SUN TEA

Fill a gallon glass jar half way with fresh, clean herb leaves, loosely packed. Fill the jar with cold water. Place in the sun and allow to steep for 4 to 6 hours. Strain out herbs before serving.

Infused Wine

Wine can be used as another liquid base to infuse herbs into. The unique flavor that wine gives will add a new dimension to salad dressing, marinades and to flavor alcoholic beverages.

 WINES FOR HERB INFUSIONS

WHITES: The most adaptable to herbs. They won't overpower herb flavors.

CHARDONNAY: Dry and fruity and mixes well with more-pungent herbs.

RHINE: Sweet and crisp and good for sweet herbs like lavender and mint.

REDS: Their stronger, lingering notes can overpower flavors and are used selectively based on the pungency of an herb.

PINOT NOIR AND CABERNET SAUVIGNON: These are the most common ones used for infusions because they tend to have a dry, less robust flavor that mixes well with some herbs.

ROSÉS: A good in-between wine compared to the lighter whites and the deep reds. They tend to be sweeter and have a refreshing note that enhances herb flavors.

WHITE ZINFANDEL: Used as a lighter version of a red wine.

Keep in mind the color of the wine infusions if you are using them in cooking – i.e., don't use reds in light-colored dishes, meats or sauces.

BASIC RECIPE FOR INFUSING HERBS INTO WINE

Start with one herb, and when experimenting, don't use more than 2 to 3 different herbs or the flavors may overpower or bitter the wine.

INGREDIENTS:

1 ounce dried herbs to 2 cups wine. If you are using fresh herbs,
   use three times the measure for dried.
Note: 1 ounce of dried herbs (approximately) is equal to ¾ cup of fine-texture fresh herbs
   like lavender flowers or chamomile (or 1 cup for bulky, whole, leafy herbs like basil and mint)

Fill a glass jar with the herbs and pour in the wine. Screw the lid on tightly and shake the mix. Allow the mix to sit in a cool, dark cabinet for a few weeks. Taste the mix to see if enough of the herb flavor has been captured in the wine. You don't want to overpower the wine with flavor, so don't leave it for too long. Strain the herbs from the wine by pouring through fine cheesecloth or cotton muslin. Rebottle.

SINGLE-HERB INFUSIONS:

REDS: Infuse with heavy, pungent herbs like rosemary, sage and thyme. Use spices like cloves, cinnamon, star anise and citrus peels.

ROSÉS: Use milder herbs like marjoram, lemon verbena, basil and lemon thyme. Use edible flowers like lavender buds and rose petals. Add vanilla beans or crystalized ginger.

WHITES: Using delicate herb flavors like lemon verbena, marjoram and mints will keep a refreshing lightness to white wines. Florals like lavender and chamomile blend well in sweet white wines like Moscato. Infuse dry wines like Sauvignon Blanc with basil, thyme or tarragon.

HERB COMBINATIONS TO TRY:

- Basil with cinnamon in a red wine
- Rose petals and lavender in a sweet white
- Rosemary and orange peels in a dry white
- Rose petals and vanilla bean in a rosé

SPARKLING WINE COOLER

PREPARATION:
Pour 1 cup of herb-infused wine into ½ cup of club soda. Add ice and garnish with a sprig of fresh herbs.

DRY WHITE BASIL AND MINT

Refreshing with the earthy aroma of basil

INGREDIENTS:
½ cup dried whole mint leaves
¼ cup dried basil
Dry white wine like a Sauvignon Blanc

PREPARATION:
Fill a glass jar with the mint and basil. Pour in the wine and stir to make sure all the herb is submerged. Screw the lid on tightly to seal the jar. Allow the mix to sit in a cool, dark cabinet for a few weeks. Taste to see if enough of the herb flavors have been captured in the wine. You don't want to overpower the wine with flavor, so don't leave it for too long. Strain the herbs form the wine by pouring through fine cheesecloth or cotton muslin. Rebottle.

BASIL MELON SMASH

INGREDIENTS:
½ cup fresh basil leaves
Cubed honeydew melon, about 1 cup
1 bottle white wine infused with basil
Juice of ½ lime

PREPARATION:
Pulse basil and melon together until mixed into a slurry liquid.
In a cocktail shaker fill half full with ice and ⅓ cup melon mix.
Shake well. Strain into a chilled glass. Pour in ⅓ cup white wine.
Squeeze in the lime juice.

SWEET WOODRUFF MAY WINE

May wine (Maiwein) is a traditional German punch served at May Day celebrations infused with the herb sweet woodruff (known in German as Waldmeister). Traditionally it is a mix of a dry white wine infused with woodruff, a sparkling wine or carbonated water and sugar. Strawberries are floated in the punch bowl because they are in season during the celebrations.

INGREDIENTS:
10 leafy stems of fresh, young sweet woodruff or about 1 cup of packed, dried leaves
1 bottle Riesling

PREPARATION:
Add the stems to the bottle of wine. Crush the leaves lightly with the handle of a wooden spoon in the liquid to release its flavor. Allow to steep a few hours or overnight, depending on how strong you want the flavor. Strain out the herb leaves.

Pour the woodruff-infused wine into a glass pitcher. Slowly pour in a dry sparkling wine until the mix is nice and bubbly. Add strawberries and fresh woodruff leaves as a garnish. Serve chilled in champagne flutes.

Herbal Cocktails & Infused Liquors

TRADITIONAL ELDERFLOWER CORDIAL

Mix with sparkling water, cocktails or wine. Splash in tea or drink warm with sliced lemons.

INGREDIENTS:

2½ cups granulated sugar

4 tablespoons honey

4 cups water

2 large lemons

10 to 15 heads of elderflower

PREPARATION:

Bring sugar, honey and water to a gentle boil over medium heat in a glass saucepan, and stir until sugar is completely dissolved. Remove from heat. Zest the lemons, then slice and squeeze the juice from them. Add the zest and juice. Carefully pick up the flowers and turn the flower heads upside down over the pan (to help keep the flavorful pollen in the mix, see Harvesting Elderflowers, next page), then drop them into the water and stir them until they are completely submerged. Cover the pan and infuse for 24 hours. Strain out the flowers and the zest through a fine mesh cheesecloth or cotton muslin. Pour syrup into a sterilized glass bottle and store in the refrigerator.

Recipe to Try:
HEDGEROW FIZZ

Elderberries are thick in hedgerows in England, and on a visit to Cornwall, I was enchanted by a drink we had at dinner. Here is my simple version of that light summery drink.

PREPARATION:

In a wine glass, squeeze in the juice of a half a lime. Add 2 to 3 tablespoons of elderflower cordial. Add chilled Prosecco to the glass, leaving a few inches from the top to splash in cold mineral water for extra fizz. Stir to mix and float fresh berries of the season.

HARVESTING ELDERFLOWERS

Harvest and use the elderflowers within a few hours of picking for best flavor. The best time is a dry, sunny day in the late morning before the hot sun releases the aroma. Cut the stalk with a sharp pair of scissors. Try to hold the flowers upright to save the pollen (where the flavor is) on the flowers. Once you have harvested a big bouquet, cut off the stems and place the flowers in a bowl or bag and shake to remove any bugs. Avoid washing the flowers because this removes too much of the flavorful pollen. A note on elderberry toxicity: The roots, stems and seeds of elderberry contain a cyanide-producing chemical that can build up in your system and cause stomach distress. Pick the flowers before the seeds have developed and don't use the leaves or stems of the plant. Cooking also removes the chemical from the flowers if there were any seeds.

MINT BOURBON

Mint julep-ready: Use this infused bourbon with a splash of mint sugar syrup (see recipe on page 124) and pour over crushed ice.

PREPARATION:

In a clean glass jar, submerge fresh mint leaves (about 20 to 25 medium-sized leaves to equal 1½ to 2 cups, packed) in a liter of bourbon. Store in a cool, dark cabinet for for about 2 weeks. Strain out the mint leaves and rebottle. Seal tightly.

BERRY HERBAL WHISKEY

No mixers needed for this: sweet and herbal, ready to sip.

INGREDIENTS:

3 pounds fresh blackberries
1 cup sugar
2 to 3 tender stems rosemary
½ cup fresh lemon verbena leaves
1 liter whiskey

PREPARATION:

In a clean glass jar, add all ingredients and shake well. Screw on the top and seal tightly. Store in a cool, dark cabinet for about 3 months. Shake the bottle every few weeks to help the sugar dissolve and the ingredients mix well. Strain out the herbs and berries and rebottle. Seal tightly.

ROSE PETAL BRANDY

Use for cooking, flavoring frosting and baked goods or as a cocktail mixer.

PREPARATION:

Collect roses in the morning just after the dew has dried. Depending on the size of the rose you may need 6 to 10 fresh roses. Prepare the petals by cutting off the bitter white end (where it was attached to the base). Fill a clean, sterilized quart glass jar loosely with the rose petals. Pour a good quality brandy in the jar and fill. It is important that the rose petals are completely submerged in the liquid. Use a bamboo skewer or chopstick to stir the ingredients together and push down any roses that float up. Cap tightly and store in a cool, dark cabinet. Shake the bottle every week. The brandy will be perfumed and flavored by the roses in about 6 weeks.

Recipe to Try:

SANGRIA

A summer classic, serve this traditional wine "punch" with fruits and herbs using a splash of your handcrafted Rose Petal Brandy. Make the recipe a day ahead to allow all the flavors to blend.

INGREDIENTS:

1 Granny Smith apple
1 orange
1 small lime
1 medium-size lemon
2 stems fresh lemon verbena
¼ cup Rose Petal Brandy
1 bottle (750 ml) dry wine like Cabernet Sauvignon
3½ cups lemon-lime soda

PREPARATION:

Prepare the fruits: Core and slice the apple into 1-inch pieces; cut the orange, lime and lemon (peel and all) into slices about ¼-inch thick. Place the prepared fruit and the lemon verbena stems in a gallon-size glass jar. Pour in the brandy and wine. Allow the mix to steep at least 2 hours or overnight for best flavor. To serve, add ice and pour in chilled lemon-lime soda.

INFUSED VODKA

Vodka is one of the best alcohols to use for herb infusions. It has a neutral flavor and easily picks up any flavor, heavy or light, that you infuse into it.

LAVENDER VODKA

INGREDIENTS:
8 stems fresh lavender
750 ml vodka

PREPARATION:
Allow to steep for a few weeks. Do a sniff test to see if the herb aroma is coming through. If not, let it steep for longer. Remove the lavender stems, strain out any remnant of lavender and rebottle.

Other herbs and flavor mixes to infuse and make your own signature herbal vodka blends:

- Lemon verbena with fresh cut lemon ribbons
- Basil and fennel
- Peppermint, spearmint or a bouquet of different types of mints
- Sweet woodruff and a vanilla bean

RECIPES

Seasoning Salts, Mixes and Grilling Rubs
Any-Herb Salt
Bouquet Garni
Brown Sugar-n-Spice Rub
Citrus Herb Pepper
Herb Garden Garlic Mix
Herbed Lime Rub
Herby Ranch Dressing Mix
Lavender French Grey sel et poivre
  (Salt and Pepper)
No-Salt Herb Blend
Peppercorn Rose Salt
Rosemary Smoked Salt
Salsa Mix
Sausage Seasoning

Signature Blends
Beef Signature Blend
Chicken Signature Blend
Dessert Signature Blend
Pork Seasoning Signature Blend
Seafood Signature Blend
Your Signature Blends

Sugars, Honey, Syrups and Jelly
Any-Herb Simple Syrup
Basic Herb Sugar Mix
Herb Honey Infusion
Lavender Simple Syrup
Lavender Lemonade
Mint Sugar
Sweet Rose Lavender Lemon
Rosemary Infused Agave
Scented Geranium Jelly
Scented Geranium Sugar

Dressing and Condiments
Basic Herb Oil infusion
Easy Oil and Vinegar Dressing
Fruit Dip
Healthy Egg-Free Salad Dressing
Herb Garden Spicy Brown Mustard
Herb Infused Mayo
Homemade Mayonnaise
Honey Butter
Honey Mustard Dipping Sauce
Ranch Dressing
Mediterranean Garden Oil
Mustard Sauce
Orange-Flavored Olive Oil
Rosemary Oil
Tarragon Mustard

Vinegars
Chive Blossom Vinegar
Basic Herb Vinegar
Basil Vinaigrette
Basil Vinegar
Dilly Zest Vinegar
Nasturtium Flower Vinegar
Orange Marjoram Vinaigrette

Sauces, Butters, Cheeses and Pastes
Basic Herb Butter
Basic Herbal Cream Cheese
Chive Butter
Flower Garden Butter
Gremolata
Herb-n-Oil Paste
Peppery Dill and Bee Balm Butter
Poppy Seed Lemon Verbena Rounds
Sweet Floral Cream Cheese

Pestos
Any-Herb Pesto
Italian Basil Pesto
Lemon Lime Pesto
Minty Sweet Pesto
Sesame Herb Pesto
Tarragon Pecan Pesto

Beverages
Herb Infused Waters:
Borage Cucumber
Cucumber Lime Mint
Fizzy Herb Water
Lavender Blueberry
Lavender Herb Soda
Pineapple Ginger
Raspberry Basil
Strawberry Lemon

Teas
Chamomile
Dill Seed
Fennel
Floral
Fresh Herb
Fresh Sun Tea
Herbal Citrus
Lemon Verbena Mint Sun Tea
Mint Geranium

Infused Wines
Basic Herb Infused Wine
Basil Melon Smash
Dry White Basil and Mint
Sparkling Wine Cooler
Sweet Woodruff May Wine

Herbal Cocktails and Infused Liquors
Berry Herbal Whiskey
Hedgerow Fizz
Herbal Hot Toddy
Lavender Vodka
Mint Whiskey
Rose Petal Brandy
Sangria
Tequila Mojito
Traditional Elderflower Cordial

Main and Side Dishes and Desserts
Easy Herb Beer Bread Mix
Easy Herbal Cheese Crisps
Geranium Lemon Tea Cake
Glazed Carrots with Lavender Honey
Healthy Pesto Bowl
Pico De Gallo
Scrambled Eggs in a Mug

Miscellaneous
Vanilla Extract
Candied Violets
Rose Water

Household and Herb Skin Care
Eco Friendly Countertop Cleaner
Lemon Verbena Epsom Bath Soak
Sea Salt Scrub

REFERENCES

A Modern Herbal, Mrs. M. Grieve F.R.H.S, revised edition, Jonathan Cape Ltd., 1973

Aromatherapy, Daniele Ryman, Bantam Books, 1993

CBS News, www.cbsnews.com/news/tongue-taste-buds-map-all-wrong/

Compound Interest, www.compoundchem.com/2014/03/13/chemical-compounds-in-herbs-spices/

Culpeper's Color Herbal, Nicholas Culpepper, David Potterton, editor, Sterling Publishing Company, Inc. 1899

Herbs (Eyewitness Handbook), Lesley Bremness, Eyewitness Books, 1994

Herbs to See, to Smell, to Taste, Susan Goetz, self-published, 1993

How to Taste, Becky Selengut, Sasquatch Books, 2018

In Love with Lavender, Susan Goetz, self-published, 2008

Mastering the Art of French Cooking, Julia Child, Louisette Bertholle and Simone Beck, updated edition, Alfred A. Knopf, 1983

Mt. Cuba Center Research Report: Monarda, www.mtcubacenter.org

Natural Food Flavors and Colorants, Mathew Attokaran, Wiley-Blackwell Publishing Ltd. and Institute of Food Technologists, 2017

Salt Works: www.seasalt.com

Sugar.org

The Complete Book of Herbs Spices and Condiments, Carol Ann Rinzler, Facts on File, 1990

The Herball, or, Generall historie of plantes, gathered by John Gerarde, www.archive.org/details/mobot31753000817749

The Spice House, www.thespicehouse.com/spices/peppercorns

USDA, (Elderberry safety reference), https://plants.usda.gov/plantguide/pdf/cs_sanic4.pdf

Web MD, www.webmd.com/vitamins/ai/ingredientmono-708/elderflower

www.ginfoundry.com/botanicals/coriander-seed/by

Other suggested reading and books from my garden library to take you further into using herbs from your garden:

Countertop Gardens, Shelley Levis, Cool Springs Press, 2018

Gardening Under Lights, Leslie Halleck, Timber Press, 2018

Herb Gardening from the Ground Up, Sal Gilbertie and Larry Sheehan, Ten Speed Press, 2012

Herbal Vinegar, Maggie Oster, Storey Publishing, 1994

Herbed Wine Cuisine, Janice Theresa Mancuso, Storey Publishing 1997

The Complete Book of Herbs, Spices and
    Condiments, Carol Ann Ronzler, Facts on File,
    1990

The Complete Herb Book, Jekka McVicar, Firefly
    Books, 2008

The Culinary Herbal, Susan Belsinger and Arthur
    O. Tucker, Timber Press, 2016

The Kitchen and Garden Book of Herbs, Jessica
    Houdret and Joanna Farrow, Southwater, 2016

The New American Herbal, Steve Orr, Clarkson
    Potter, 2014

Herb Publications

Herb Quarterly, www.herbquarterly.com

Mother Earth News, www.motherearthnews.com

Mother Earth Living, www.motherearthliving.com

Herb Societies and Information Sources

American Botanical Council,
    www.herbalgram.org

Herb Research Foundation, www.herbs.org

Herb Society of America, www.herbsociety.org

International Herb Association, www.iherb.org

North Carolina State University, www.ncherb.org

Other Media

Garden Therapy, www.gardentherapy.ca

Living Homegrown, www.livinghomegrown.com

INDEX

RESOURCES

Dried herbs and kitchen supplies

Frontier Natural Products Co-op
800-669-3275
www.frontiercoop.com
Dried herbs and spices in bulk, tea supplies, press and seal tea bags, bottles.

Mountain Rose Herbs
800-879-3337
www.mountainroseherbs.com
Dried herbs and spices in bulk, tea supplies.

Starwest Botanicals
800-800-4372
www.starwest-botanicals.com
Dried herbs and spices in bulk, tea supplies, cooking oils, flavor extracts.

Crystalized Citrus
www.truelemon.com

Packaging

SKS Bottle and Packaging
519-880-6980
www.sks-bottle.com

Freund Container and Supply
www.freundcontainer.com

World Market
www.worldmarket.com

Sur La Table
84 Pine Street, Seattle Washington
and many cities.
www.surlatable.com

Plants and Seeds

Shop your local garden stores and farmers markets first!

Botanical Interests
www.botanicalinterests.com

Ed Hume Seeds
www.humeseeds.com

Hudson Valley Seeds
www.hudsonvalleyseed.com

Johnny's Selected Seeds
www.johnnyseeds.com

Mountain Valley Growers
559-338-2775
www.mountainvalleygrowers.com

Renee's Garden Seeds
888-880-7228
www.reneesgarden.com

Richter's Herbs
905-640-6677
www.richters.com

Seed Savers
www.seedsavers.org

Territorial Seed Company
800-626-0866
www.territorialseed.com

ACKNOWLEDGMENTS

Thank you to those who encourage my work by reading my books and social media posts and coming to my talks and workshops about herbs. It is joy for me to hear about how you get excited and explore more about what you grow in the garden.

In the work of this book, writing at a computer for hours on end can be a lonely job but the process of putting a book together is not. Many people come and go, and woven in the writing of this are pieces of inspiration – a photograph, a conversation with a fellow herb lover or a walk through a garden.

Thank you to Sass Ruthven with Share the Wealth Organics in Tacoma, Washington, for letting me come by to photograph and pick herbs in your abundant gardens. Thank you to my daughter Courtney for helping with photography (and testing the recipes after we were done photographing!) To my dear friend Mison, who has always been an encourager and one of the most talented flavorful cooks I know: You inspire me by your passion for flavor from food.

To the St Lynn's Press family: Thank you to Paul Kelly for giving me the opportunity to share my love for herbs in another book. I am so very grateful to your talented team. Cathy, thank you for your calming and reassuring voice on the phone and wonderful crafting of my words. To Holly: Every time I get to see a plain Word document come to life on the pages you design I am mesmerized by how you transform it all. Thank you all for your time and care you take to publish beautiful books.

And of course, last but not least, to my girls. Alyssa, Hayley and Courtney. Three beautiful women who encourage and support me in all the twists and turns we take in life. I am truly blessed.

ABOUT THE AUTHOR

Sue Goetz is an award-winning garden designer, writer and speaker. *A Taste for Herbs* is her second book to celebrate her love of growing and creating with herbs from the garden. Her first was *The Herb-Lover's Spa Book* (St. Lynn's 2015).

Through her business, Creative Gardener, she works with clients to personalize outdoor spaces – from garden coaching to full landscape design. A popular speaker and hands-on workshop leader, Sue is all about creativity in and out of the garden.

Her garden design work has earned gold medals at the Northwest Flower & Garden Show and specialty awards, including; the *Sunset* magazine award, the *Fine Gardening* magazine award and The American Horticultural Society Award. She has been named Educator of the Year by the Washington State Nursery and Landscape Association and shares her love of the garden and herb growing all over the U.S. A member of GWA (The Association of Garden Communicators), her work has appeared in numerous publications, including the *Tacoma News Tribune, Seattle Met,* and *APLD Designer, Pacific Horticulture,* and *Fine Gardening* magazines.

Sue lives in the beautiful Pacific Northwest and when not up to her nose in herbs and dirt in the garden she enjoys creating collaged art with pressed plants and botanical illustration.

Connect!
www.thecreativegardener.com
www.herbloversgarden.com
Facebook.com/CreativeGardener
Pinterest: Sue Goetz
Instagram: creativegardener
Twitter: @gardenersue
Linked In: Sue Goetz

Other books from St. Lynn's Press

www.stlynnspress.com

The Herb Lover's Spa Book
by Sue Goetz
192 pages • Hardback
ISBN: 978-0989268868

The Foodscape Revolution
by Brie Arthur
192 pages • Hardback
ISBN: 978-1943366187

Simple Pleasures
by Chris Fennimore & Daniel Agüera
192 pages, Hardback
ISBN: 978-1943366323

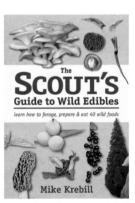

The Scout's Guide to Wild Edibles
by Mike Krebill
192 pages • Paperback
ISBN: 978-1943366064